THE COOKIE BIBLE

Publications International, Ltd.

Favorite Brand Name Recipes at www.fbnr.com

Microwave Cooking: Microwave ovens vary in wattage. Use the cooking times as guidelines and check for doneness before adding more time.

Preparation/Cooking Times: Preparation times are based on the approximate amount of time required to assemble the recipe before cooking, baking, chilling or serving. These times include preparation steps such as measuring, chopping and mixing. The fact that some preparations and cooking can be done simultaneously is taken into account. Preparation of optional ingredients and serving suggestions is not included.

contents

cookie fundamentals

Who doesn't love cookies?
Cookies are the universal crowd-pleasing treat—irresistibly sweet, conveniently portable and so much fun to eat. What other food could welcome children home from school, take center stage at community bake sales, and help celebrate countless holidays and special occasions?

Fortunately, baking cookies is not difficult, and the rewards can go far beyond just a batch of homemade goodies: Baking cookies can create wonderful memories, establish family traditions, bring friends together, and even relieve stress!

The information that follows is designed to help you get started. It may seem overwhelming, but the actual details are very simple. If you need to know the difference between types of flour, what to look for when purchasing cookie sheets, or how to cream butter or separate an egg, the answers are all right here.

Start with the simplest cookies and work your way through the tremendous variety of recipes offered in *The Cookie Bible.* The journey—and the results—will be delicious!

ingredients

The first rule of baking cookies is the simplest one: Stock your pantry with basic and frequently used ingredients. The information that follows will help you learn what ingredients you might need and any important details about purchasing them and storing them for maximum freshness. With the right ingredients always on hand, it's easy to make fabulous cookies at a moment's notice.

Flour

Flours are categorized by the grain from which they come and, in the case of wheat flour, by the variety of the grain and the processing method used. Wheat flour, the most commonly used flour for making cookies, is harvested from the tiny berries on wheat stalks. (Other grains, such as oats, rice, barley, rye and buckwheat, are also milled into flours, but these are not often used in baking.) All wheat flours contain gluten, a protein that is activated when dough is mixed and is important in providing the structure in baked goods. Gluten amounts vary with the type of wheat: Soft wheat has a low gluten content and is used in cake flour, while hard wheat has a high gluten content and is used in bread flour. Several types of wheat flour are typically available at the supermarket:

All-purpose flour is a blend of hard and soft wheats. It contains only the center of the wheat kernel, not the germ (the heart) nor the bran (the outer coating). Wheat flour naturally whitens through oxidation if allowed to age for a month or two, resulting in a slight cream color. Bleached all-purpose flour is whitened with hydrogen gas and benzoyl peroxide or other chemical agents; its color is pure white. Bleached and unbleached all-purpose flour can be used interchangeably in cookie recipes. Most all-purpose flour comes presifted, eliminating the need to sift unless specified in a recipe.

Store all-purpose, cake and bread flour in airtight containers in a cool, dark place for up to six months. Temperatures above 70°F encourage bug infestations and mold, so if your kitchen is too warm, or for longer storage, refrigerate or freeze flour in moistureproof wrapping. Flour can be stored in the freezer for up to one year. (Allow chilled flour to return to room temperature before using it.)

It's best to transfer dry ingredients such as flour and sugar to airtight containers after opening them, because storing them in their original packaging can attract insects such as mealy bugs and ants. Always clean the storage container before adding new flour, and don't pour fresh flour on top of old flour.

Whole wheat flour is milled from the entire wheat kernel; it is coarser and denser than all-purpose flour with a greater gluten content and higher nutritional value. It is generally used in combination with all-purpose flour in cookie batters and doughs, producing a dense, chewy cookie with a nutty flavor. Whole wheat flour is more perishable than other flours, so purchase it in small amounts and store it in the refrigerator for up to three months.

Cake flour is made from soft wheat flour and is used to produce delicate pastries and cakes. It is usually available at the supermarket in two-pound boxes, sometimes in both plain and self-rising varieties. Be sure

to purchase the plain cake flour, as the self-rising cake flour has leavening and salt added to it. If a recipe calls for cake flour and you don't have any on hand, you can substitute one cup all-purpose flour less two tablespoons for each cup of cake flour required.

Cornmeal

Cornmeal is made from dried corn kernels. There are two grades: coarse, used for polenta and for cornmeal mush; and fine, ground from white, yellow or blue corn and used in baking, as a coating, and occasionally as a thickener. Fine grade is more common. Either grade can be stone-ground, in which the whole corn kernels are ground between two enormous water-powered stones. This results in a meal that has more vitamins and nutrients than electric-milled commercial cornmeal; it is coarser in texture and more flavorful, but also more perishable—it should be stored in the refrigerator for up to three months or in the freezer for up to one year.

Commercial steel-ground cornmeal, produced by a modern electric milling process that removes the husk and germ, is more finely textured and is the variety typically found in supermarkets and used in cookie recipes. Store steel-ground cornmeal in an airtight container in a cool, dry place for up to one year.

Cornstarch

Cornstarch is a smooth powder made from the endosperm (center) of dried corn kernels. It is used primarily as a thickener for sauces and custards, but it is sometimes mixed with all-purpose flour to create cookies that are more tender and lighter in texture.

Cornstarch is available in boxes in the baking section of the supermarket, and it can last indefinitely when stored in a cool, dry place.

Oats

Oats are one of the most nutritious of grains, high in protein and fiber. Whole oats must be processed

before they can be eaten— they are cleaned, toasted, hulled, steamed and finally flattened into flakes. Old-fashioned rolled oats are larger and coarser in texture than quick-cooking rolled oats; they don't absorb as much moisture so they produce slightly moister, chewier and more rustic-looking cookies. Quick oats are essentially the same oats that have been rolled into thinner flakes so they have a finer texture, cook faster and absorb moisture better.

Old-fashioned oats and quick oats can be used interchangeably in most cookie recipes unless the recipe directs otherwise; however, the finer texture of

quick oats makes them especially good for no-bake cookies.

Oats are sold in cardboard containers in the cereal section of the supermarket; they should be stored airtight at room temperature for up to six months. Be careful not to confuse the different varieties of oats available. Instant oatmeal is not the same as quick-cooking oatmeal and should not be used for baking. Scotch oats, steel-cut oats and Irish oatmeal are oats that have been cut into pieces but not rolled. They are used to make cereal but are not good for baking because of their very coarse texture and the length of cooking time required.

Leaveners

Leaveners react with liquids to create air bubbles in dough, causing cookies to puff up. Cookies usually call for one or two types of leaveners: baking soda and/or baking powder. They are not interchangeable, but both need to be somewhat fresh to be effective. Check the expiration date on the containers; the leavening power may be very limited or entirely gone if the product is older than the date on the label.

Baking powder is a leavener made of baking soda, cream of tartar and a small amount of cornstarch (to stabilize the mixture). When mixed with liquid ingredients, baking powder releases carbon dioxide gas bubbles that cause cookies and other baked goods to rise. Almost all baking powder found in American markets is double acting—it releases some gas when it is first mixed with liquids, then releases the rest when heated in an oven. This double action means that batters and doughs can stand for a while before going into the oven without losing their leavening power, a useful property when making several batches of cookies.

Cookies made with baking powder bake more quickly, spread less and do not brown as well as cookies made with baking soda. To test if your baking powder is still effective, stir one teaspoon into $\frac{1}{2}$ cup hot water. If it fizzes, it's still good. If your cookies turn out flat, however, it is not necessarily the fault of old baking powder—too much baking powder can actually cause your cookies to deflate rather than rise, and it will also leave them with a chalky taste. One teaspoon per cup of flour is the standard amount.

Baking soda, also called bicarbonate of soda, has four times the leavening power of baking powder; only a small amount is needed to make batters rise. (The standard amount is $\frac{1}{4}$ teaspoon per cup of flour.) Because baking soda is alkaline, it releases carbon dioxide bubbles when combined with an acidic ingredient such as buttermilk, brown sugar, molasses, honey, sour cream, fruit or chocolate. Baking soda should always be mixed with other dry ingredients first because it reacts immediately when wet; this is also why batters and doughs containing baking soda should be put in the oven as soon as possible after mixing—so the rising takes place in the oven rather than in the mixing bowl.

Baking soda is often added to cookie recipes as a color enhancer rather than as a leavener. Since acidic doughs don't brown well, baking soda is added to neutralize their acidity and create better browning.

Cream of tartar is a fine white powder that is a component of baking powder; it is sometimes used with baking soda as a leavener for cookies. (It is actually an acid made from the residue found inside wine tanks or casks after fermentation.)

Cream of tartar is used most often to stabilize egg whites and achieve maximum volume while whipping them; it is also added to frosting and candy mixtures for a creamier texture. Cream of tartar is sold in small jars in the spice section of supermarkets; it keeps indefinitely if stored in a cool, dry place.

sugars and other sweeteners

All sweeteners are carbohydrates derived from the roots, stems or leaves of plants. Sweeteners do more than just add sweetness to cookies—they improve tenderness, texture and color, and also help cookies stay fresher longer. The most commonly used sweetener is sugar, most of it coming from sugar cane or sugar beets.

Brown sugar, a blend of granulated white sugar and molasses, has a soft, moist texture and distinctive flavor. It comes in two varieties, light and dark. Light brown sugar contains less molasses, has a lighter color and a more delicate flavor than dark brown sugar. Some brown sugar is not labeled light or dark—if the package only says "brown sugar," it is light brown. Both types add moisture, flavor and color to cookies; they can be used interchangeably in most cookie recipes but you may notice a difference in the results: Dark brown sugar will give cookies a stronger flavor and darker color.

Brown sugar dries out and hardens quickly when exposed to air, so the package should be sealed as tightly as possible after opening. Storing the package inside an airtight container and/or in the refrigerator also helps to keep brown sugar moist. The freshness of the brown sugar does affect the texture of the finished cookies—using hardened sugar produces a dough that is less creamy and cookies that become dry when cool. If your brown sugar does become too hard to measure, it can be softened in the microwave oven. Heat one cup brown sugar at High for 30 seconds, watching to make sure it doesn't begin to melt. Repeat the process if necessary.

Granulated white sugar is the most common variety of sugar in cookie recipes. It is highly refined into tiny white grains, readily available in bags and boxes, and keeps indefinitely stored in an airtight container in a cool, dry place.

Powdered sugar, also called confectioners' sugar, is granulated sugar that has been ground into a powder and mixed with a small amount of cornstarch (1 to 3 percent) to prevent caking and keep it dry. The package may also include the words "10X sugar," which means that the sugar was processed to a fineness ten times that of granulated sugar—this is the finest powder and what is sold in supermarkets. Other grades of sugar exist, such as 4X and 6X, but they are only used by professional bakers and confectioners.

Powdered sugar dissolves easily and is most often used in frostings and glazes and to dust the tops of cookies; however, it is also used in some cookie and bar recipes to produce cookies with a very tender texture and tight crumb. As powdered sugar is less sweet and much lighter in texture than granulated sugar, the two are not interchangeable in recipes. Powdered sugar should always be sifted before using, since even a new package still tends to have clumps.

Corn Syrup

Corn syrup is a thick, sweet and highly refined liquid made by treating cornstarch with acids and enzymes that cause it to liquefy. It comes in two varieties: Light corn syrup has been clarified; it is clear and almost flavorless. Dark corn syrup has caramel flavoring and color added; it has a stronger, molasses flavor. They can be used interchangeably unless a recipe directs otherwise.

Corn syrup adds moisture to cookies, helps them brown more quickly and stay fresher longer. It is also invaluable in making candy and frostings since it prevents sugar from crystallizing. (Sugar crystals make candy and frostings grainy and coarse.) Corn syrup is sold in glass jars and should be stored at room temperature.

Honey

Honey is a thick, sweet, golden liquid manufactured by honeybees from the nectar of flowering plants. (Liquid honey is actually extracted from the honeycomb by centrifugal force, then heated, strained, filtered and often pasteurized.) Its flavor and color vary depending on where the honey was produced and the type of flowers the bees fed on. The most common types of honey available in supermarkets come from the nectar of clover, orange blossom or lavender flowers, although a wide range of different flavors are increasingly available at gourmet

stores and farmers' markets. Generally, the darker the color, the deeper the flavor.

Honey keeps indefinitely if stored in a sealed container in a cool, dark and dry place; however, it does darken with age and become a bit stronger in flavor. Honey may also develop sugar crystals but these do not indicate any deterioration of the honey. It can be easily liquified by placing the open container in a pan of hot water or microwaving the open container at High for 20 to 60 seconds. (The water temperature should not exceed 160°F, as temperatures hotter than this will alter the flavor of the honey.) Honey adds flavor and moisture to cookies and contributes to a softer, chewier texture. Honey also attracts moisture from the air, so cookies made with honey may become even softer in storage.

Maple Syrup

Maple syrup comes from the sap of certain species of mature maple trees. A tap inserted into the tree trunk during sugaring season drains the sap, which is then boiled and concentrated to form the thick, sweet liquid known as maple syrup. It is graded according to color: the lighter the color, the higher the grade and the more delicate the flavor. Once opened, maple syrup should be refrigerated to prevent mold from forming. If it crystallizes, it can be liquified by heating the open container in a pan of warm water or in the microwave oven. Maple-flavored syrup is a mixture of a less expensive syrup, usually corn syrup, and maple syrup. Pancake syrup is artificially flavored.

Molasses

Molasses is a thick, dark, strong-flavored liquid that is a by-product of the sugar refining process, obtained after the sugar cane juice has been boiled until it crystallizes to become table sugar. The liquid remaining is molasses. Molasses taken after the first boiling is called first strike, or light; it is the highest quality, sweetest and best for table use. The liquid may be boiled again to extract more sugar; the resulting molasses is called second strike, or dark, a good choice for baking.

Light and dark molasses can be used interchangeably in recipes. Blackstrap molasses, the darkest and thickest, is taken after the third boiling. It has a bitter flavor and is generally not recommended for baking purposes. Sulfur is sometimes used in the processing of sugar cane juice, resulting in a darker molasses with a more pronounced flavor. Molasses should be refrigerated after opening.

fats, eggs and dairy

Fat is absolutely essential in cookie baking—it contributes flavor and moisture to cookies and also helps maintain freshness. There are several different types of fat used in baking; each has different properties that affect the texture and flavor of your cookies. For the best results, always use the type of fat specified in the recipe.

Butter

Made from cream, butter is about 80 percent butterfat and 10 to 16 percent water. (The rest is milk solids.) Butter is scored by the United States Department of Agriculture (USDA) and assigned quality grades based on flavor, body, texture, color and salt. Grade AA (93 score) is the highest grade and the most common grade available in the retail market. Butter is usually sold in one-pound packages that contain four (4-ounce) sticks, both in unsalted and salted varieties. Unsalted butter is preferred by many bakers, as it has a fresher, sweeter flavor and less moisture, and

it allows the consumer to control the salt content of a recipe. Although it varies by manufacturer, salted butter has about 1½ teaspoons added salt per pound. Some experts recommend reducing the amount of salt in a recipe if you are using salted butter.

Cookies made with butter spread more than cookies made with shortening; they generally come out more crisp and of course, have a buttery flavor. Whipped butter should never be used for making cookies—it has too much air beaten into it and will not produce good results. Similarly, reduced-calorie and reduced-fat butters should be avoided, since they have a higher water content and will greatly affect the texture of the cookies.

Butter should be stored in the refrigerator and used on or before the expiration date stamped on the package. Keep it tightly wrapped, covered and away from strong-flavored foods because it easily picks up other flavors and odors. Refrigerate butter for up to ten days, or store it in the freezer for up to six months, with the original packaging wrapped in plastic wrap or placed in resealable plastic freezer bags.

Margarine

Margarine is a solid fat made from hydrogenated vegetable oils (usually corn or soybean oil), along with skim-milk solids, emulsifiers, salt and preservatives. (The hydrogenating process means that pressurized hydrogen gas is forced through liquids to change them to solids.) By law, margarine must contain at least 80 percent fat; products with less than that amount are labeled spreads and are not recommended for baking because of their high water content.

Margarine is softer and more oily than butter and is available in similar one-pound packages that each contain four sticks. It should be stored in the refrigerator for up to one month or in the freezer for up to six months. Stick margarine, or stick margarine-butter blends (usually 60 percent margarine and 40 percent butter), can be substituted for butter in most recipes. However, the resulting flavor and texture of the cookies may be different, especially in recipes where butter is the primary ingredient.

Shortening

Shortening is 100 percent fat, made from soybean, corn, cottonseed, palm or peanut oil that is processed with heat and hydrogen. Available in cans and sticks, the original variety is pure white and flavorless, while butter-flavored shortening is yellow colored with artificial flavoring added.

Because shortening does not contain water, it melts at a higher temperature than butter, causing cookies made with shortening to spread less quickly (or not at all) and end up puffier than cookies made with butter. Shortening can be used interchangeably with butter, but the flavor and texture of the cookies may be very different. Shortening remains solid at room temperature and can be kept, covered or wrapped, for up to one year. Storing shortening in the refrigerator will help it stay slightly fresher and whiter, but it is not necessary.

Vegetable Oils

Vegetable oils, such as canola, corn, safflower or soybean oil, are all 100 percent fat. These oils can be used in baking—they provide moisture and tenderness—but are not very common in cookie recipes. Most recipes that use oil call for part oil and part butter, margarine or shortening; cookies made with this combination of fats often turn out flat with crackly or crinkled tops.

When a recipe does call for oil, choose a mild, neutral-flavored oil like those listed above. Peanut and olive oils have distinctive flavors that may not work well in cookies. However, the flavor of olive oil is an essential part of many Mediterranean baked goods, so if a recipe calls for olive oil, do not substitute another vegetable oil in its place. Also, do not substitute vegetable oil for solid shortening, as the consistency of the dough will be drastically affected. Store oils in a cool, dark place for three to six months. (Heat, light and time will turn oils rancid.)

Eggs

Eggs are an essential ingredient in most cookies. Egg yolks, high in fat, contribute richness, tenderness and color to cookies, while protein-packed egg whites add structure, stability and moisture. Eggs are sold by grade and size. The grade of an egg is not the measure of its freshness but is based on attributes, such as thickness of the white, firmness of the yolk and size of the interior air pocket. There are three grade classifications for eggs: AA, A and B. High-grade eggs (AA) have firm, compact, round yolks with thick whites—these are the best eggs for baking. The color of the egg shell (white or brown) is determined by the breed of the chicken and does not affect flavor, quality, nutrients or cooking characteristics of the egg.

There are six size classifications for eggs—jumbo, extra-large, large, medium, small and peewee—determined by the minimum weight allowed per dozen. Most recipes that call for eggs are developed using large eggs, so use large eggs when making cookies unless the recipe specifies otherwise.

Select clean, unbroken eggs from refrigerated cases and always purchase eggs as fresh as possible. The USDA requires that egg cartons display the packing date, which is indicated by a number representing the day of the year. For example, January 1 is day 1 and December 31 is day 365. An expiration date (month and day) may also be displayed. This is the last sale date and must not exceed thirty days after the packing date. Refrigerate eggs immediately after purchasing and store them in the coldest part of the refrigerator, in their original carton, with the pointed ends facing down. Don't store eggs in refrigerator egg bins or open containers, as eggshells are porous and can easily absorb odors and bacteria from other foods.

A very small percentage of American eggs are contaminated with salmonella, a bacteria that causes a type of food poisoning. It is important to handle eggs properly to avoid illness caused by this bacteria. Keep eggs refrigerated until shortly before using them. If a recipe calls for room temperature eggs, remove only the number of eggs needed and let them stand on the counter for no more than 30 minutes before using.

Do not eat raw eggs or foods containing raw eggs, which for cookie bakers means you should not taste any dough or batter with eggs before it is baked. After handling raw eggs, wash your hands before touching other food or equipment, and keep your equipment and counter surfaces clean to avoid cross-contamination. If you have serious concerns about handling raw eggs, pasteurized eggs in the shell are now available in many supermarkets. The pasteurization process removes the risk of salmonella, while allowing eggs to taste and function like regular (unpasteurized) eggs. Because of this extra processing, pasteurized eggs are more expensive.

Egg substitutes are made almost entirely with egg whites (about 80 percent), plus artificial color and stabilizers. With no egg yolks, egg substitutes don't behave the same way as eggs do in baking—at the minimum, cookies come out drier using egg substitutes, and there may be other differences as well.

Milk

Whole milk contains about 3½ percent milkfat, while the low-fat varieties contain 2 percent or 1 percent. Skim milk has less than ½ percent milkfat. Unless specified, whole, 2 percent and 1 percent milks are interchangeable in cookie recipes. Skim milk is too thin and will not produce good results.

Cream

Cream is the thick part of milk that contains a rich concentration of butterfat. Different types of cream are based on their percentage of butterfat. Whipping cream, or heavy cream, has 35 to 40 percent butterfat or occasionally more. Light cream contains about 20 percent fat, although the fat content can go as high as 30 percent. Half-and-half, made from equal parts cream and milk, has 10½ to 15 percent butterfat. If a recipe calls for a specific type of cream, then it is best to use that type; otherwise, the fat content of the cookie will change and the texture will be affected.

Almost all whipping cream found in supermarkets today is ultrapasteurized, a process of heating that considerably extends the shelf life of cream by killing bacteria and enzymes that cause milk products to sour. Store cream in the coldest part of the refrigerator as soon as possible after purchasing; most types will last about a week beyond the "sell by" date on the container.

Buttermilk

Originally buttermilk was the liquid left over after butter was churned, but now it is made commercially by adding lactic acid bacteria to milk. Buttermilk has a slightly thickened texture and tangy flavor, and it imparts this rich taste and tenderness to baked goods. Buttermilk powder is a convenient product available in some supermarkets; a mixture of milk and vinegar or lemon juice added can also be substituted for buttermilk for use in baking. (See Bakers' Substitutions, page 53.)

Cream Cheese

Cream cheese is a soft, unripened cheese made from cow's milk. By law cream cheese must contain at least 33 percent milkfat and no more than 55 percent moisture; it also contains gum arabic (a colorless, odorless and tasteless natural additive) to increase its firmness and shelf life.

Cream cheese is sold in three- and eight-ounce packages in the dairy case of the supermarket; it should be stored tightly wrapped in the refrigerator and used within a week after opening. (Be sure to check the date stamped on the package before purchasing.)

Cream cheese adds tenderness to cookies; it is often used in combination with butter to produce a rich, delicate dough. Do not substitute reduced-fat or fat-free cream cheese for the regular version unless a recipe suggests it. Whipped cream cheese cannot be used for baking either, as the air whipped into it makes it lighter in volume than regular cream cheese.

flavorings

From spices and extracts to chocolate, fruits and nuts, there are numerous ingredients cookie bakers should have on hand to create a wide range of fabulous cookies.

Spices

Spices are the aromatic parts of plants, such as bark, berries, buds, flowers, fruit, roots or seeds. Unlike herbs, which are outdoor plants that can grow in many climates, spices come from plants that thrive in tropical regions. Spices should be stored in a cool, dry place in tightly covered lightproof containers. Do not keep them above the range, as heat and moisture will cause their flavor to deteriorate more quickly. Most spices are available ground or whole; ground spices should be purchased in small quantities since they lose their flavor and aroma very quickly.

Allspice is the dried, pea-size berry of the evergreen pimiento tree. The dark brown berries are available whole or ground and taste like a combination of cinnamon, nutmeg and cloves.

Cardamom is a member of the ginger family, available in pods (which contain seeds), whole seeds or ground. It has a pungent aroma and an intense spicy-sweet flavor. Use it sparingly, since a little goes a long way.

Cinnamon comes from the dried bark of various laurel trees. The outer bark is peeled away, then the inner bark is rolled, pressed and dried. Cinnamon comes in two varieties (from different trees): Cassia cinnamon is the spice most commonly found in supermarkets (simply labeled cinnamon); it has a strong, warm, bittersweet flavor. Ceylon cinnamon has a mildly sweet, fresher flavor. Cinnamon is available in sticks (often used to flavor beverages) or ground.

Cloves are the dried, unopened flower buds of the tropical evergreen clove tree. Cloves are reddish brown in color, have a strong sweet flavor and resemble small nails. They are available whole or ground.

Ginger has several different forms and a multitude of uses. Fresh ginger is a gnarled, tan-colored root that adds its own distinctive pungency and aroma to foods. It is used extensively in Asian and Indian cooking. Dried ground ginger has a very different flavor and is not an appropriate substitute in recipes calling for fresh ginger—it is more frequently used in baked goods such as cookies, cakes and breads, but it is added to savory dishes as well.

Nutmeg is the inner brown seed of a tropical evergreen tree. It has a spicy-sweet flavor and aroma and is available whole or ground. The nutmeg seed is covered with a lacy membrane that is dried and ground, becoming the subtler flavored mace. Use freshly grated nutmeg whenever possible—it is much more flavorful than ground, and easy to produce with an inexpensive nutmeg grater.

Peppercorns are the dried berries of the pepper plant family. Black peppercorns are the strongest and spiciest type; they are made from unripe berries fermented for several days before drying. Used sparingly, pepper can add an exciting flavor boost to cookies, especially when paired with chocolate. Peppercorns are sold whole, cracked or ground, and, as is the case with other spices, freshly ground pepper will provide far more flavor than pre-ground.

Salt

Salt is an important ingredient in cookies, mainly serving to enhance the flavor of other ingredients. Use the amount of salt called for in the recipe—too much may give your cookies an unwanted salty flavor, and too little may cause the recipe not to work properly. Table salt is the most common form of salt and the one that should be used in baking; it is fine-grained and contains additives that prevent it from clumping. Salt will keep indefinitely when stored in a cool, dry place.

Vanilla

Vanilla is the pod fruit of the tropical vanilla orchid. Obtaining vanilla beans is very time consuming and labor intensive, which is the reason that pure vanilla has remained relatively expensive throughout history. The orchid flowers must be hand-pollinated, then mature pods are later hand-picked before beginning a tedious six-month curing process. Pure vanilla extract is made by steeping these cured vanilla beans in a solution of at least 35 percent alcohol, water and sugar, which acts as a preservative.

Imitation vanilla is made entirely of artificial flavorings. It can have a harsh quality that pure vanilla doesn't have, and it may leave a bitter aftertaste. Products labeled "vanilla flavoring" are a combination of pure and artificial vanilla extracts.

Like all extracts, vanilla is very concentrated and should be measured carefully. It should not be added to hot liquids, as some of the vanilla flavor will evaporate along with the alcohol. Vanilla extract will keep indefinitely when stored tightly capped in a cool, dark place. (If the cap is not sealed tightly, the extract will evaporate quickly due to the alcohol content.)

Flavored Extracts

Other extracts, such as almond, mint, lemon and orange, are concentrated flavorings derived from these foods by distillation or evaporation. Usually pure extracts are preferred over the synthetic versions, but the imitation flavors can be used if necessary.

Coffee

Both coffee and espresso, in their granulated or powdered forms, can add wonderful flavor to cookies. Freeze-dried instant coffee works fine in recipes, and instant espresso powder can be found in some supermarkets, gourmet shops or Italian grocery stores. Both products are usually dissolved in a small amount of liquid before mixing with other ingredients. The exact amounts and directions should be specified in the recipe.

Chocolate

Chocolate comes from the cocoa bean, which is produced by cocoa trees in tropical climates. After the harvest, cocoa beans are fermented for several days, dried in the sun and then shipped to processing centers where they are roasted and cracked open to separate the shells from the kernels, or "nibs." Nibs are over 50 percent cocoa butter (a natural vegetable fat) that melts when the nibs are ground, producing a thick, dark brown liquid called chocolate liquor. The chocolate liquor may then be pressed, extracting much of the cocoa butter to form dry, hard cakes which are ground into cocoa powder. Or, the chocolate liquor may undergo certain blending and refining processes, when such ingredients as sugar, cocoa butter and condensed milk may be added to make different types of chocolate.

Chocolate should be stored, tightly wrapped in foil or brown paper, in a cool, dry, dark place, between 60° and 70°F. If stored at room temperature, the cocoa butter melts, rises to the surface and resolidifies. This causes the chocolate to develop a "bloom," or a pale gray film on the surface. If stored in a damp place, the chocolate can form tiny gray sugar crystals on top. These conditions only affect the appearance, but not the flavor, of the chocolate—the rich brown color will return when the chocolate is melted.

Ideally chocolate should not be kept in the refrigerator (where it will pick up moisture), but this may be unavoidable if your kitchen is very warm and humid. Stored properly, bittersweet and semisweet chocolate will last for several years. Because they contain milk solids, white chocolate and milk chocolate have a much shorter shelf life and should be used within about nine months.

Unsweetened chocolate, also called baking chocolate, is pure chocolate with no sugar or flavorings added. It is used only in baking and is commonly packaged in individually wrapped one-ounce squares.

Bittersweet chocolate is pure chocolate with some sugar added. It is available in specialty food shops and some supermarkets, packaged in chips, bars or one-ounce squares. If unavailable, substitute half unsweetened chocolate and half semisweet chocolate.

Semisweet chocolate is pure chocolate combined with extra cocoa butter and sugar. Available in chips, chunks, bars and one-ounce squares, it is interchangeable with bittersweet chocolate in most recipes.

Milk chocolate is pure chocolate with sugar, extra cocoa butter and milk solids added. With a milder flavor than other chocolate, it is widely used for candy bars and is also sold in various shapes such as chips and stars. Milk chocolate cannot be used interchangeably with other chocolates because the presence of milk changes its melting and cooking characteristics.

White chocolate is not considered real chocolate since it contains no chocolate liquor—it is a combination of cocoa butter, sugar, milk solids, vanilla and emulsifiers. White chocolate is available in bars, blocks, chips and chunks. Some products labeled "white chocolate" do not contain cocoa butter but are simply coatings, so check the ingredient list for cocoa butter to make sure you have the real thing.

Unsweetened cocoa powder is formed by extracting most of the cocoa butter from pure chocolate and grinding the remaining chocolate solids into a powder. When cocoa powder is further treated with alkali to help neutralize cocoa's natural acidity, it produces a dark, mellow-flavored powder called Dutch-processed cocoa that is preferred by many baking professionals. The two types of cocoa are often interchangeable in recipes, but there will be some differences in color and flavor—baked goods made with Dutch-processed cocoa will be somewhat milder in flavor and darker in color. Cocoa powder can be stored in a tightly closed container in a cool, dark place for up to two years.

nuts, dried fruit and seeds

Nuts add flavor, texture and visual interest to cookies. You'll get the freshest flavor if you purchase whole nuts and chop or grind them yourself, but many varieties of nuts are conveniently available in the form in which they will be used (chopped, ground or slivered). When purchasing nuts in bulk, taste a nut first to make sure that it's fresh—a rancid or stale flavor means the nuts are no longer good, and a few bad nuts can spoil a whole batch of cookies.

When purchasing nuts in their shells, look for clean, unbroken shells without cracks or splits. Nuts should feel heavy for their size and appear well shaped, with no holes or cracks in their shells. Shelled nuts should be plump, crisp and uniform in size and color.

Nuts are usually chopped or ground and sometimes toasted before adding to cookie dough. A small quantity of nuts can be chopped with a chef's knife on a cutting board; for larger amounts it is easier to chop them with a food processor fitted with a steel blade. Use on and off pulses when chopping, being careful not to keep the machine running too long. (Most nuts have a high oil content and can easily turn to paste or nut butter when ground.) To reduce the risk of overprocessing, add a small amount of the flour or sugar from the cookie recipe. Recipes usually call for either coarsely chopped nuts, which are pieces between ¼ and ½ inch in size, or finely chopped nuts, which are about ⅛-inch pieces.

Nuts should be stored in a cool, dark place until opened. After opening, store nuts in a tightly sealed container in the refrigerator for up to three months, or in the freezer for up to one year. (If you purchase nuts with no plans to use them right away, store them in the freezer.)

Almonds are oval, flat white nuts with thin brown skin and light tan pitted shells. There are two types of almonds, bitter and sweet. The bitter variety contains toxic prussic acid when raw. The acid is destroyed by heating, so commercial processors use this stronger flavored almond to make extract and liqueurs. Sweet almonds have a delicate, slightly sweet flavor and are used for baking and cooking. They are available blanched (skins removed) and unblanched (raw with skins intact, also called "natural"), whole, sliced, slivered and chopped.

Cashews are the seeds of a tropical fruit called a cashew apple. The nut is kidney-shaped with a sweet, buttery flavor and crunchy texture. Cashews contain about 48 percent fat, so they tend to turn rancid quickly. Store them airtight in the refrigerator to prolong their shelf life.

Hazelnuts or filberts have a sweet, rich flavor and thin brown skin that is usually removed before eating. One way to remove the skin is to place the nuts on a baking sheet and bake them in a preheated 350°F oven for 7 to 10 minutes or until the skin begins to flake off. Remove the nuts from the oven, wrap them in a heavy towel and rub them against the towel to remove as much of the skin as possible. To save time when baking, hazelnuts can also be purchased, whole or chopped, with the skin already removed.

Macadamia nuts have an extremely hard brown shell with cream colored meat and a buttery rich, slightly sweet flavor. They are the world's most expensive nut because they are so labor-intensive to produce. Macadamia nuts are usually sold shelled, either roasted or raw. They are also very high in fat, so they are best kept refrigerated or frozen to prevent them from turning rancid.

Peanuts are actually legumes, similar to peas, but they have pods that ripen underground. Oval-shaped Virginia peanuts and small, red-skinned Spanish peanuts are the most common varieties. Peanuts have ivory-colored flesh and a buttery flavor that is intensified by roasting. Shelled peanuts are typically packaged in vacuum-sealed cans or jars; they are usually roasted and available salted or unsalted. Recipes will specify which type to use.

Pecans are a sweet, rich nut with smooth tan shells that are thin but hard. Pecans are available shelled and unshelled, in halves, pieces or chips. With the highest fat content of any nut, pecans should be stored airtight in the refrigerator or freezer to prevent rancidity.

Pistachio nuts have a hard tan shell which is sometimes dyed red or blanched until white, and the inside meat has a pale green color and a delicate, subtly sweet flavor. Pistachios are sold in many forms: shelled and unshelled, salted and unsalted, raw and roasted. Shelled pistachio nuts are the most convenient form for baking, but if unavailable, purchase nuts in plain-colored (not red) shells that are slightly open, an indication of ripeness.

Walnuts are available in many varieties, but the most common is the English walnut. It has a mild flavor and a light brown shell that is ridged and oval in shape. Make sure the shelled walnuts you purchase for baking look plump and feel crisp (they should snap when broken); shriveled walnuts are stale and may taste bitter.

Dried Fruit

Coconut is the fruit of the coconut palm tree. The most common type of coconut used in cookies is packaged sweetened coconut, available in bags or cans, shredded or flaked. Unsweetened coconut is sold in similar forms but can be somewhat harder to find; it is usually sold in health food stores. Be sure to use the type of coconut that the recipe calls for. Unopened packages of coconut can be stored at room temperature for up to six months. After opening, both types should be stored in a tightly sealed container in the refrigerator or freezer to retain freshness.

Dried cranberries are increasingly popular in cookie recipes, contributing a chewy texture and a pleasant sweet-tart flavor. Available in packages or in bulk, dried cranberries should be stored in an airtight container at room temperature for up to several months, or in the refrigerator for longer storage.

Currants are produced from drying tiny seedless Zante grapes. They are generally much smaller and drier than raisins, but the two are interchangeable in cookie recipes.

Raisins are simply dried grapes, usually Thompson seedless grapes. Like other dried fruit, raisins have a chewy texture and very sweet flavor due to their high natural concentration of sugar. They add sweetness, moisture and texture to cookies. Dark raisins are sun-dried for several weeks so they end up dark and shriveled, while golden raisins are dried with artificial heat and treated with sulphur dioxide, leaving them lighter-colored and plumper. Available in cardboard boxes or in bulk, raisins should be stored in an airtight container at room temperature for several months, or in the refrigerator for up to a year.

Seeds

Anise seeds come from a plant that is a member of the parsley family. The oval, greenish-brown seeds have a delicate sweet licorice flavor similar to fennel. The seeds are a popular ingredient in many European and Mexican confections, as well as in savory dishes in a variety of cuisines around the world. The seeds are available whole or ground; purchase whole seeds for the best flavor and grind them just before using.

Poppy seeds are the very tiny bluish-grey to black ripe seeds of the opium poppy plant, which is native to the Mediterranean region. They add a nutty flavor and crunchy texture to cookies and other baked goods, and they are frequently used in Middle Eastern, Indian and Central European cooking. Poppy seeds have a high oil content, so they should be stored airtight in the refrigerator or freezer.

Sesame seeds are the seeds of a leafy green plant native to East Africa and Indonesia. These tiny round seeds are usually ivory colored, but brown, red and black sesame seeds are also available (for use in cooking rather than baking). Sesame seeds, regardless of color, have a slightly sweet, nutty flavor. They are widely available packaged in supermarkets and are sold in bulk in specialty stores and ethnic markets. Because of their high oil content, they easily turn rancid and are best stored in the refrigerator for up to six months or in the freezer for up to a year.

Sunflower seeds come from the huge centers of the sunflower plant. The seeds are oval shaped with a hard black-and-white or grey-and-white striped shell. The shell is removed and only the kernel of the seed is eaten. The kernels, which are referred to as seeds, may be dried or roasted and salted and used like nuts in baked goods. Like other seeds, sunflower seeds are high in fat, so they should be stored in the refrigerator to prevent them from becoming rancid. Dried or roasted seeds will keep up to four months.

equipment

Can equipment really make a difference in baking cookies? The short answer is yes. What holds true for so many different activities also applies to baking: Having the right tools makes it much easier to succeed. The good news is that baking cookies doesn't require a lot of equipment when you're just getting started, and many of the items you need may already be in your kitchen for general cooking and baking purposes.

Make sure that what you do purchase is the best quality you can afford—these items may cost a little more, but they are worth the investment since they will produce better results and last longer. And when you look over this list, remember that you don't need to own everything, only the tools to make the kind of cookies you want to bake.

Measuring Cups

All bakers need two types of measuring cups. Dry measuring cups are used for ingredients such as sugar and flour, as well as for solid shortening. They come in sets of nested and graduated cups made of metal or plastic, including ¼ cup, ⅓ cup, ½ cup and 1 cup measures. (Some sets may also include the in-between sizes such as ⅛ cup, ⅔ cup and ¾ cup as well.) Dry measuring cups do not measure liquids accurately.

Liquid measuring cups are, as the name implies, just for measuring liquids. They are available in glass, plastic and metal, but clear glass is the most practical choice—you can see the liquid you are measuring and it is a heatproof material. Liquid measuring cups have calibrations marked on the side, a small pouring spout and a handle opposite the spout; they come in 1-cup, 2-cup and 4-cup sizes.

Measuring Spoons

Measuring spoons come in nested sets of ¼ teaspoon,

½ teaspoon, 1 teaspoon and 1 tablespoon. (Some larger sets also include ⅛ teaspoon and 1½ teaspoons.) Available in metal or plastic, measuring spoons are used to measure small amounts of either dry or liquid ingredients. Do not substitute the teaspoons and tablespoons from your everyday silverware to measure ingredients; these spoons don't hold the same amount as measuring spoons.

Mixing Bowls

It's a good idea to have at least a few sizes of mixing bowls on hand, made of stainless steel, glass and/or ceramic. (Plastic bowls are not as practical because they are porous and may retain oils and odors.) Deep bowls with high sides are especially useful if you will be using a hand mixer, and pouring spouts are helpful for handling thinner mixtures like brownie batter.

Spatulas

Rubber spatulas, sometimes called scrapers, are flexible utensils with a paddlelike rubber, plastic or nylon head attached to a handle. They come in a wide variety of sizes and are ideal for scraping out the insides of bowls, containers and measuring cups. The larger ones are also good for folding and mixing dough. Some of the newer rubber spatulas are

heatproof, which are wonderful to use when melting chocolate; however, they are not as flexible as regular spatulas so they are not as good for mixing purposes.

Long narrow metal spatulas are useful for leveling off dry ingredients when measuring them and for loosening edges of cookies and bars that are stuck firmly to the pan.

Wide flexible metal spatulas, also called cookie turners or pancake turners, are a necessity for removing baked cookies from cookie sheets. These spatulas have a solid, flat, square or rectangular metal blade attached to a handle. The spatula should be wide enough to slide under and pick up a whole cookie without it hanging over the edges of the blade. The thinner the metal, the easier it is to slide under cookies without breaking or mangling them. For very thin, delicate cookies, it is essential that the metal part of the spatula be thin, but that isn't as important with sturdier cookies like chocolate chip or oatmeal raisin.

Mixing Spoons

Every kitchen needs a few good mixing spoons for stirring mixtures on the stove or mixing ingredients by hand. Wooden spoons are the most popular option, as they are sturdy and comfortable to hold, and along with plastic spoons, they can be used on nonstick surfaces. Keep in mind that wood is a porous material that absorbs odors, so it's a good idea to keep separate spoons for sweet and savory cooking. Select spoons that are stamped from a single piece of material because joints break over time and are more difficult to clean. Wooden spoons will last longer if they are not subjected to the dry heat of the dishwasher.

Whisks

Made of stainless steel wires that loop to form a bulbous shape, wire whisks are designed to aerate and mix. Larger balloon-type whisks are used for whipping air into ingredients such as egg whites and cream, while small and medium whisks are used for stirring hot mixtures as they cook and blending ingredients together without beating a lot of air into the mixture. Select whisks with sturdy wires and handles that are easy to grip.

Knives

Good-quality knives are important in baking as well as cooking, but only a few of them are used with regularity. A chef's knife has a wide, slightly curved blade from seven to twelve inches long; it is used for most chopping tasks (such as nuts, dried fruit or chocolate) and for slicing rolls of dough. A paring knife has a short two- or three-inch-long blade and is used for peeling and slicing fruit, cutting out garnishes and other small jobs. A long serrated knife is useful for cutting biscotti dough into slices.

Sifter

A flour sifter consists of a fine mesh screen and a mechanism to push flour through the mesh. Sifting aerates dry ingredients such as flour, powdered sugar and cocoa powder; it also breaks up lumps and gives dry mixtures a uniform consistency. A sifter with a two- or three-cup capacity and a crank-type handle is a good choice, but a strainer can be used instead if you don't have a sifter. Never wash a sifter; just wipe it out with damp paper towels.

Graters

A four-sided box grater is a versatile and inexpensive tool with several different size openings; it can be used for grating citrus peel and chocolate in addition to its more common functions, grating cheese and vegetables. Smaller graters with handles may be easier to use and more convenient for baking jobs—these can be kept in a drawer or hung on a hook with other utensils.

A nutmeg grater is another inexpensive little tool that is helpful to bakers, since so many cookie recipes call for nutmeg, and the flavor of freshly grated nutmeg is far superior to that which is already ground. These metal graters are about four inches long, two inches wide and the shape of a half cylinder with a fine grating surface on the curved part of the tool.

Double Boiler

A double boiler consists of two stacked pans. The top pan, which holds food, nestles in the bottom pan, which holds an inch or two of simmering water. (The bottom of the top pan should never touch the water—it should only be warmed by the steam.) The purpose of a double boiler is to protect heat-sensitive foods like chocolate from direct heat.

You can easily make your own double boiler by setting a stainless steel bowl over a pot of simmering water. Chocolate can be melted by other methods—in a heavy saucepan over direct heat or in a microwave oven—but a double boiler is the safest way to do it (there is less chance of burning the chocolate).

Pastry Blender

This hand-held tool consists of several U-shaped wires or metal blades attached to a handle. It is used to cut butter or shortening into flour, which is an essential step in making some cookie doughs and most pie doughs. Two knives can also be used to accomplish the task if you don't have a pastry blender on hand.

Rolling Pin

Rolling pins are used to roll out cookie dough before it is cut into shapes. They can be made from hardwood or marble, or sometimes from metal or plastic. The typical American rolling pin is made of wood, has a handle on each end and rolls on bearings. The French version has no handles. A heavy rolling pin allows for the most efficient rolling, because the weight of the pin does most of the work, requiring less effort from the user. Wood rolling pins should be wiped clean with a dry cloth (rather than washed) to prevent warping.

Pastry Brushes

Pastry brushes are small, flat brushes made of natural bristles, such as boar bristles, or nylon. They are primarily used to apply melted butter or glazes to cookies before or after baking, but they are also useful for brushing off excess flour from doughs and even for buttering the insides of baking pans. Brushes should be washed by hand with hot, soapy water, rinsed well, then air dried after reshaping the bristles. Nylon bristles tend to tear dough and may begin to melt when they come in contact with heat; boar bristle brushes are more expensive but last longer.

Scoops

Stainless steel ice cream scoops with squeeze handles are used not only for portioning ice cream but also for portioning cookie dough or other batters. They create perfectly uniform cookies (which can be difficult to do using spoons) and keep your hands clean in the process. Scoops come in a variety of sizes and are labeled with a number from 8 to 100—the smaller the number, the larger the bowl of the scoop. (This number indicates the number of scoops that can be made from one quart of ice cream.) Good sizes for cookie batter are 40, 50, 70 and 80.

Cookie Cutters

Cookie cutters made of metal or plastic cut decorative shapes from cookie dough. The cutters come in an enormous variety of shapes and sizes (often in nested or themed sets) with quality ranging from thin and flimsy to solid and sturdy. Wash and dry cookie cutters well after each use, and store them in separate containers or boxes (away from other utensils) so they won't get bent or crushed.

Pastry Bag

A pastry bag is a cone-shaped bag made of canvas, plastic or plastic-lined cloth. It is used to pipe foods, such as frosting, whipped cream, cookie dough or batter, in a decorative pattern. It is open at both ends. The food to be piped is placed in the larger opening, while the smaller opening is fitted with decorative tips made of plastic or metal. The bag is squeezed to force the contents through the tip.

Larger pastry bags fitted with plain or star tips are typically used to pipe out cookies (like meringues) and fillings for sandwich cookies; smaller bags are often used for decorating. (A small, resealable plastic food storage bag with a tiny hole cut from the corner of the bag can also take the place of a pastry bag for simple decorating.) A quick alternative to a pastry bag for decorating cookies is a plastic squeeze bottle—filled with melted chocolate or icing, it can make drizzling and decorating easier, especially for the novice.

Parchment Paper

Parchment is heavy paper that is impervious to grease and moisture. It is sold in sheets and rolls at gourmet kitchenware stores and at many supermarkets. When used to line cookie sheets, parchment paper provides a nonstick surface and allows for effortless removal of cookies (and makes cleanup very easy). Parchment paper can also be made into cones that function as disposable pastry bags to pipe icing or chocolate onto cookies.

Oven Thermometer

Actual oven temperatures frequently vary quite a bit from the dial setting, so it is essential to keep a good-quality mercury oven thermometer in your oven all the time and adjust the dial setting to compensate as necessary. Most home ovens are off between 5 and 50 degrees, and sometimes even more. If your oven temperature isn't correct, your cookies will be underbaked or overbaked.

Timer

A timer is extremely helpful when baking cookies, especially for baking more than one batch at a time. Many ranges, ovens and microwave ovens have built-in timers that can do the job. Free-standing timers are also available; they come in a range of styles and prices.

Cookie Sheets

The number of different cookie sheets to choose from can be overwhelming. The best cookie sheets to use are those with little or no sides, which allow the heat from the oven to circulate easily during baking and promote even browning. Choose ones made of heavy-gauge aluminum that are light in color. Thin cookie sheets can warp and buckle in the oven; dark ones absorb more heat and bake cookies too quickly, which can cause cookies to be too dark and/or dry. (If you do have thin cookie sheets, you may stack two sheets together for added insulation.)

Nonstick cookie sheets are not a good choice for all-purpose cookie baking. Many cookie recipes call for using ungreased cookie sheets, and if you use nonstick cookies sheets for these recipes, the coating on the nonstick cookie sheets will cause cookies to spread too much. They can be used successfully for recipes that call for greased cookie sheets—but do not grease them, as the nonstick coating takes the place of greasing.

Insulated cookie sheets, also called cushioned or double layered, are another option that some bakers prefer while others do not like. They have a layer of air sandwiched between two layers of aluminum, intended to promote even baking and prevent the bottoms of cookies from burning. You might find that cookies take longer to bake on these sheets; they may also brown less overall and be more difficult to remove from the cookie sheets because the bottoms are more tender. Avoid using them if you are making cookies that you want to be crisp.

Keep the size of your oven in mind when purchasing cookie sheets. Make sure there is at least two inches of oven space around them so the heat can circulate well and your cookies will bake evenly. If possible, have three or four cookie sheets on hand so while one sheet is in the oven, you can always be getting another one ready to go.

Baking Pans

Most of the properties of a good cookie sheet are also desirable in a baking pan: It should be made of sturdy aluminum for good heat conduction, and be shiny or light in color to reflect heat away from the cookies and prevent the crust from becoming too brown and hard.

Jelly-roll pans, sometimes called half-sheet pans, are shallow aluminum pans with a very low rolled rim. They measure $15\frac{1}{2} \times 10\frac{1}{2} \times 1$ inch or $17 \times 11 \times 1$ inch in size and are used to make thin sheet cakes and some bar cookies. They are not the best option for individual cookies because the sides interfere with air circulation during baking, resulting in uneven browning.

Most bar cookies are baked in square or rectangular metal baking pans—either 8×8, 9×9, 11×7 or 13×9 inches—with sides at least $1\frac{1}{2}$ inches high. Bar cookies may also be baked in glass baking pans and dark nonstick pans; if you use these, you should reduce the oven temperature by 25 degrees and check for doneness at least 3 minutes before the recipe's minimum baking time to prevent overbaking. (Glass conducts heat faster than aluminum and dark pans absorb more heat than shiny ones.)

Cooling Racks

A cooling rack is a raised wire rack used to cool baked goods. It is raised to allow air circulation around the

baked goods or baking pan, which speeds cooling and prevents steam accumulation that results in soggy cookies. Choose stable racks that are at least ½ inch high for good circulation, with the metal wires close together so very small or delicate cookies don't fall between them.

Another option is a wire mesh rack (with small square grids) that provides more support and eliminates the problem of cookies slipping between the wires. Both types of cooling racks come in a variety of sizes and shapes (rectangular, square or round); they are also available with a nonstick coating. Whatever type you select, have several racks on hand to accommodate a few batches of cookies at the same time.

Electric Mixers

An electric mixer is not essential, but if you bake cookies often, it does make the process a lot quicker and easier. Stand mixers are considerably more expensive, with a solid base, a heavy-duty motor and several adjustable speeds. They can handle larger quantities of dough and mixtures that are more dense.

Most mixers come with one bowl and the basic mixing attachments, such as a flat beater and a wire whip. If you frequently bake more than one type of cookie at a time, it is helpful to have an extra bowl and another set of attachments so you don't have to stop and wash dishes in the middle of baking. (The extra set is also useful when you need a separate bowl to beat egg whites or whip cream.)

Hand-held mixers have two removable beaters attached to plastic or metal housing that holds the mixer's motor. They can do most of the operations of stand mixers and offer the convenience of portability, but they sometimes have difficulty with heavy doughs. (They also leave you with only one free hand.)

Food Processors

A food processor can be used for mixing doughs and batters, but it is not always the best tool for this job. Its ability to produce good cookie dough will depend on the age and capacity of the machine, the size of the motor and the sharpness of the blade; you should consult the manufacturer's directions for making cookie dough in the food processor. What it does do very well is chop, slice, shred and purée—these tasks can be done in a fraction of the time it takes to do them by hand.

techniques

Measuring

The first step to successful cookie baking is the careful measuring of ingredients. Unlike cooking, baking requires that recipes be followed exactly—a little too much of one ingredient or not enough of another really does make a difference in the final results.

To measure flour, first spoon it into a dry measuring cup until it is mounded over the rim, then level off the top with a straight-edged knife or spatula. Don't shake or tap the measuring cup or press the flour down; this compacts the flour and you may end up with too much, ultimately resulting in dry or crumbly cookies. If a recipe calls for "sifted flour," sift the flour before it is measured. If a recipe calls for "flour, sifted," measure the flour first and then sift it.

Sugar is measured differently depending on the type of sugar you are using. For granulated sugar, simply dip the measuring cup into the container of sugar, then level off the excess as described above. Brown sugar must be packed down until it is level with the top of the measuring cup for an accurate measurement. To test if you've filled the cup properly, turn it upside down—if the sugar holds its shape, it's been correctly measured. Powdered sugar should be spooned into a measuring cup and leveled off like flour.

To measure liquid ingredients, place a liquid measuring cup on a flat surface and add the liquid until it reaches the correct amount. Make sure you read the measurement line at eye level; reading it from above looks different and will result in an inaccurate measurement.

It is easiest to measure thick, sticky liquids such as corn syrup, maple syrup, molasses and honey in dry measuring cups. Spray the measuring cup with nonstick cooking spray (or lightly grease it with vegetable oil) before measuring so the syrup will slide right out and not stick to the cup.

Stick butter and margarine have measurement markings right on the wrapping. Be sure to look carefully at the markings before cutting the amount you need, because they are not always positioned correctly— sometimes the start of the markings is not aligned with the beginning of the stick. Vegetable shortening should be measured just like brown sugar, packed into a dry measuring cup (to eliminate any air pockets), then leveled off at the top with a straight-edged knife or spatula. Shortening is also sold in packages of one-cup sticks, with measurement markings on the wrapper similar to butter. Vegetable oil should be measured in liquid measuring cups.

Temperature

For the best results, your ingredients should be at or near room temperature before baking unless a recipe directs otherwise. This helps create a well-blended, more homogeneous dough.

Butter should be slightly firm; it should give gently to pressure. (Too-soft butter will create overly soft dough, and cold butter will not blend well with the other ingredients.) It can be softened quickly in the microwave oven if necessary: Heat butter for 15-second intervals using Low (30% power), checking it after each interval. Vegetable shortening and oil can be used immediately if stored at room temperature; they should stand at room temperature for about 15 minutes if they have been stored in the refrigerator.

Remove eggs from the refrigerator 20 to 30 minutes before baking to bring them to room temperature. If you don't have the extra time, you can place the (whole) eggs in a bowl of lukewarm water for several minutes.

Working with Eggs

When adding eggs to a recipe, crack one egg into a separate bowl before adding it to the mixing bowl, and repeat this process with each egg. This prevents any egg shell fragments from getting into the batter; it also prevents a spoiled egg from ruining the batter. Once the eggs have been added, scrape down the side of the bowl to make sure they are fully incorporated into the batter. Don't worry if the mixture looks a bit curdled after adding the eggs; it will smooth out after the dry ingredients are added.

Eggs separate more easily when they are cold. You can separate eggs with your hands or an inexpensive gadget called an egg separator, but the most common method is to use the two egg shell halves. To separate an egg yolk from the white, gently tap a clean egg in the center with a table knife or against a hard surface, such as the side of a bowl. Carefully break the egg in half over a small bowl. Holding an egg shell half in each hand, gently transfer the yolk back and forth between the two shell halves, allowing the white to drip into the bowl. Place the yolk in another bowl. Transfer the egg white to a different bowl before separating another egg.

If the egg yolk breaks while separating the egg, try not to let any yolk drip into the bowl with the egg white; this will prevent the egg white from whipping up to its full volume. (To remove any traces of yolk, use a cotton swab or the corner of a paper towel.) When recipes call for beaten egg whites, start with room temperature egg whites. Always check that the bowl and beaters are clean and dry, as the smallest trace of yolk, fat or water can prevent the whites from obtaining maximum volume. Do not use plastic bowls, because they may have an oily film even after repeated washings.

Beat egg whites slowly with an electric mixer at low speed until the whites are foamy. Then gradually increase the speed to medium-high. (A gradual increase helps beat air in slowly and give the egg whites a stronger structure.) Add a pinch of salt or cream of tartar to stabilize the foam, and continue beating until the egg whites reach

the desired stage. Stop the mixer often to look at the egg whites so you don't end up overbeating them. At the soft peak stage, the egg whites should be fluffy, moist and shiny looking; when the beater is lifted, the egg white peaks curve slightly. This takes about 3 to 4 minutes with a stand mixer. At the stiff peak stage, egg whites are glossy and hold their shape easily—the peaks stand straight up. This takes about 5 to 6 minutes with a stand mixer. Watch carefully when approaching the stiff peak stage, as it's easy to overbeat the whites. They will become dry, then lose their volume and fall apart into a lumpy, watery foam. Beaten egg whites should be used immediately so their volume is not lost.

Melting Chocolate

Chocolate is a delicate ingredient, so it is essential to melt it carefully. Bars and chunks of chocolate should always be broken or chopped into small pieces to ensure even melting—this helps retain the flavor and texture of the chocolate. (Small pieces melt quickly and have less chance of burning, while large pieces can melt unevenly, with the surface area overheating before the center melts.) Chop chocolate, a small amount at a time, on a cutting board with a chef's knife. A food processor is not a good tool for this purpose because the heat of the motor can melt the chocolate.

Semisweet and dark chocolate should be stirred frequently during melting, but milk and white chocolate must be stirred almost constantly because the milk solids they contain are very sensitive to heat. The utensils used for melting must be completely dry—any moisture will cause chocolate to become stiff and grainy (a condition called "seizing"). Never cover chocolate during or after melting; this can result in drops of condensation mixing with the chocolate. If the chocolate does seize, add ½ teaspoon shortening (not butter) for each ounce of chocolate and stir until smooth.

Methods of Melting

Double boiler: This is the safest way to melt chocolate. Place the chocolate in the top of a double boiler or in a bowl over hot, not boiling, water; stir gently until the chocolate is smooth. Make sure that the water level in the bottom pot is at least an inch from the bottom of the top pot, and keep the heat low. (Boiling water turns to steam, which will condense and mix with the chocolate, causing it to seize.) When removing the top part of the double boiler, wipe the bottom and side dry so that no stray drops of water mix with the chocolate when it is transferred to a bowl.

Direct heat: Place the chocolate in a heavy saucepan over very low heat. Stir constantly and remove from the heat as soon as the chocolate is almost melted. Continue stirring until it is completely melted. Use the lowest heat possible and watch the chocolate carefully—it scorches very easily with this method, and once chocolate is scorched, the flavor is ruined and it cannot be used.

Microwave oven: Place four to six unwrapped one-ounce squares or one cup of chocolate chips in a small microwavable bowl. Microwave at Medium (50% power) 2 to 3 minutes, stirring after the first minute and then at 30-second intervals until the chocolate is smooth. (It is very important to stir microwaved chocolate between heating intervals because it retains its original shape even when melted, and it can fool you into thinking it is not melting.) To prevent the risk of overheating, remove the chocolate from the microwave when it is almost melted, then stir and let any small undissolved lumps finish melting at room temperature.

Chocolate can also be microwaved at High 1 to 1½ minutes, stirring at 30-second intervals until smooth. However, when melting white or milk chocolate, it is safer to use Medium, as these chocolates are more heat-sensitive and can burn very quickly. No matter which level of heat you choose, you should check the chocolate frequently—melting times will vary depending on the wattage of your microwave and the amount of chocolate you are melting.

Toasting Nuts

Toasting nuts before using them intensifies their flavor and crunch. To toast nuts, spread them on a baking sheet and place in a 350°F oven for 8 to 10 minutes, shaking the pan several times. (The time will vary depending on the amount of nuts, the size of the pieces and the oil content of the nuts.) You can also toast nuts in an ungreased skillet over medium heat until golden brown, stirring frequently. With either toasting method, watch the nuts carefully—their high fat content means they burn easily, and burnt nuts have a bitter taste that will ruin a recipe. Always cool nuts to room temperature before combining them with other ingredients.

Toasting Coconut

The full flavor of shredded coconut is released when it is toasted. Spread the coconut in an even layer on a baking sheet and place it in a preheated 350°F oven for 8 to 10 minutes, stirring occasionally to ensure even browning. If the coconut is fresh and moist, it will take a little longer to reach a rich golden color than drier coconut. The coconut will become crisper as it cools.

Preparing Dried Fruit

Cranberries, raisins or any other dried fruit in a recipe should be moist when you use it. If the fruit is too dry, it is easy to plump it by placing the fruit in a small bowl and covering it with warm water. Let it soak for 30 minutes and drain well before using. If you don't have that much time to wait, this step can also be done quickly in the microwave: Place ½ cup dried fruit and one tablespoon water in a microwavable bowl, cover with plastic wrap and heat at High for about 30 seconds. Allow the fruit to stand about 1 minute before draining well and proceeding with the recipe.

Larger pieces of dried fruit, such as apricots, must be chopped before adding them to a batter; this is easy to do on a cutting board with a chef's knife. Spray the knife with nonstick cooking spray or lightly coat it with oil to prevent the fruit from sticking. If you don't have a large quantity of dried fruit to chop, you can also cut it into small pieces with kitchen scissors.

Preparing Pans

When it comes to preparing pans for baking, it is very important to follow the recipe directions. Cookie sheets should be greased only if the recipe requires it—many cookie doughs contain a high percentage of fat and can be baked on an ungreased pan without sticking. (The less fat a cookie contains, the more likely the cookie sheet will need greasing.) There are several options to consider when greasing cookie sheets: butter, shortening, oil or nonstick cooking spray. Some bakers like to use butter for the flavor, while others believe that butter, margarine and oil make the area between cookies more likely to burn during baking so they prefer shortening instead.

Nonstick cooking spray is a convenient option, but it can sometimes leave an unpleasant residue on the pan, particularly when used with insulated cookie sheets. Whatever option you choose, avoid overgreasing; this will cause cookies to spread too much and overbrown the bottoms. Nonstick cookie sheets should never be greased even if the recipe calls for greasing, as this can also cause cookies to spread too much.

Parchment paper is an excellent alternative to the greasing options listed above. Baking cookies on parchment paper ensures their easy removal; it also helps cookies retain their shape, bake evenly and prevent overbrowning—and it makes cleanup a breeze. If a recipe calls for parchment paper, this means that the cookies are particularly fragile or sticky and using parchment paper best facilitates their removal from the cookie sheet. To prevent the paper from curling up or slipping around, use a very small piece of dough in each corner of the cookie sheet to "glue" the parchment down.

Bar cookie and brownie recipes often call for greased baking pans; these pans can be greased just like cookie sheets. Parchment paper is not recommended for square and rectangular baking pans; however, aluminum foil does an excellent job of keeping pans clean and making bars and brownies easy to remove.

A quick and easy way to line a baking pan with foil is to invert the pan and shape the foil over the bottom. Lift the shaped foil off and fit it into the upright pan. Make sure there is at least a two-inch overhang of foil on each side to use as handles for lifting out the bars after baking. If the recipe calls for a greased baking pan, the foil should be greased (which can be done easily with nonstick cooking spray).

Preheating the Oven

It is a simple but very important step: Always preheat the oven to the proper temperature. Cookies placed in a cold oven will not bake properly. Preheating an oven takes about 10 minutes, so usually you should turn on the oven when you begin making the dough. The exception is with refrigerator cookies, or other cookies that require dough to be chilled; in those cases you should turn on the oven 10 minutes before you are ready to bake.

Making the Cookies

Cookie recipes and techniques may vary, but a few guidelines apply to cookie baking in general:

- Read the entire recipe before beginning to make sure you have all the necessary ingredients and baking utensils.
- Unless a recipe directs otherwise, have all ingredients at room temperature, so they can combine more readily and produce a smoother dough.
- Toast and chop nuts, peel and slice fruit, and melt chocolate before preparing the cookie dough.
- Add ingredients to the batter gradually or in stages so they blend in better (and you won't end up with a batter that is grainy from sugar not incorporating properly or bits of flour left at the bottom of the bowl).

- Avoid overmixing batter or dough; this can result in cookies that are tough or dry or spread too much.
- Create cookies that are uniform in size and shape so they finish baking at the same time.
- For even baking and browning, position an oven rack in the center of the oven and only bake one cookie sheet at a time. If you do use two sheets at one time, rotate them from top to bottom and front to back halfway through the baking time to facilitate more even baking. Position oven racks close to the center to prevent the tops and bottoms of the cookies from burning.
- Remember that cookies will continue baking after being removed from the oven (from the heat retained by the cookie sheets); take this into account when checking for doneness.
- Allow cookie sheets to cool between batches; the dough will spread if placed on a hot cookie sheet.

Drop Cookies

These cookies are named for the way they are formed on the cookie sheet. The soft dough mounds when dropped from a spoon then flattens slightly during baking. Recipes will indicate what amount of dough to use—usually a teaspoon or a tablespoon—and for forming cookies, regular flatware can be used instead of measuring spoons since these measurements don't need to be so precise.

Drop the dough from the tip of the spoon (rather than the side) for a well-rounded cookie. Use a second spoon

or a small spatula to push the dough onto the cookie sheet. Space the mounds of dough about two inches apart on the cookie sheets to allow for spreading unless the recipe directs otherwise.

To portion out dough evenly, use an ice cream scoop with a release bar. They come in various sizes and make it easy to form cookies of the same size and shape. (A #70 scoop holds about one tablespoon of dough; a #80 scoop holds about one teaspoon.)

If the dough becomes too soft in a warm kitchen or while standing between batches, just refrigerate it for several minutes until it firms up again. You can also chill dough to make slightly thicker cookies that spread less, but don't allow the dough to become too hard. For softer cookies, remove them from the oven when they are still slightly underbaked.

Hand-Formed or Shaped Cookies

These cookies can be simply hand-shaped into balls or crescents, forced through a pastry bag or cookie press into more complex shapes or baked in cookie molds. For evenly proportioned hand-formed cookies, scoop out the dough with a spoon before shaping it. When rolling cookie dough into balls, roll each ball no more than three or four times between your palms—overworked dough becomes too soft and will not hold its shape during baking. If the dough sticks to your hands, coat your hands lightly with flour or sugar, or dampen them with cold water periodically. Try to keep your hands cool, so they don't warm up the dough and cause it to spread.

Some hand-formed cookie recipes call for pressing down on the balls of dough with the bottom of a glass before baking. This flattening helps ensure the cookies are a uniform thickness, and when the glass is dipped in sugar, adds additional texture to the cookies. Hand-formed peanut butter cookies are traditionally flattened with a fork in a decorative criss-cross pattern.

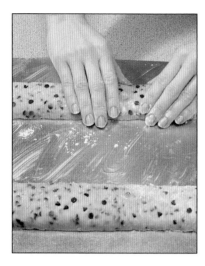

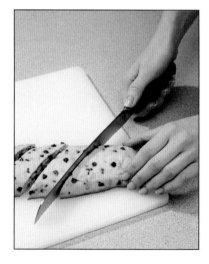

Biscotti are traditional Italian cookies that are partially shaped by hand and baked twice. (The dough is first formed into logs and baked, then the logs are cut into slices and the slices are baked.) Biscotti dough does not spread much, so you can shape the dough into two logs on one large cookie sheet or jelly-roll pan. The exact dimensions of the logs vary with the recipe.

Biscotti logs are done when they are lightly browned and the top is firm to the touch. Let them rest for at least 10 minutes before slicing, usually on the diagonal, with a serrated knife. When slicing, cut down while drawing the knife towards you instead of moving the knife back and forth as you do when slicing bread. Biscotti slices then go back in the oven to bake as the recipe directs (usually about 10 minutes per side) until they are crisp and lightly browned.

Cutout or Rolled Cookies

These cookies are made from stiff doughs that are rolled out and cut into shapes with cookie cutters, a knife or a pastry wheel. This dough is always chilled in the refrigerator or freezer after mixing; chilling changes the texture of the dough and makes it firmer and easier to handle. But the dough cannot be too cold, or it will crack and be difficult or impossible to roll. If the dough becomes too cold, let it stand at room temperature for a short time until it yields to the touch.

Divide the dough into several smaller pieces before chilling it, and wrap each piece separately in plastic wrap. It is much easier to work with a small portion of dough at a time, and the dough is less likely to become too soft. Keep the remaining portions of dough wrapped in the refrigerator until you are ready to use them.

To roll out dough, you need a smooth surface, a rolling pin and all-purpose flour. Generally the surface, the rolling pin and the dough should be dusted lightly with flour before beginning. Roll dough from the center out to the edges, then lift the rolling pin and bring it back to the center—don't roll back and forth because this toughens the dough. Give the dough a quarter-turn periodically to make sure you're rolling it to an even thickness. Moving the dough around and turning it over occasionally also helps prevent it from sticking. If the dough does stick to the work surface, carefully loosen it with your fingers or a metal spatula, then dust the surface and the dough lightly with flour. It may be necessary to flour the dough several times while you're rolling before it no longer sticks, so make sure you sprinkle the flour very lightly—too much flour incorporated into the dough will make it tough. A pastry brush is helpful for brushing excess flour from the dough.

For dough that is extremely soft or sticky, you may prefer a slightly different method of rolling. Roll out the dough between two sheets of lightly floured waxed paper, occasionally lifting the waxed paper off the dough to make sure it isn't sticking and dusting the dough with additional flour if necessary. This technique can be used with all rolled-out doughs; it makes cleanup very easy.

When cutting out cookies, press down firmly on the cookie cutter so it cuts all the way through the dough. Press straight down to make a clean cut; avoid twisting the cookie cutter in the dough. Dip the cookie cutter in flour every two or three cookies to prevent sticking, making sure to shake or tap off any excess flour. Make each cut as close as possible to the previous cut to

minimize the amount of dough wasted.

Don't roll out the scraps of dough immediately—wait until you have the leftover dough from each portion you roll out and press them all into a ball. Chill this dough briefly before rolling it out and cutting more cookies. It's best to only re-roll dough one time, because the dough (and the resulting cookies) will get tougher with each rolling. Transfer the cookie cutouts to a cookie sheet with a wide metal spatula.

Refrigerator Cookies

These cookies are made from dough that is shaped into logs, refrigerated until firm and then sliced for baking. When preparing the dough, keep in mind that ingredient pieces such as nuts and fruit should be finely chopped for easier slicing. To shape the dough, first place it on a piece of waxed paper or plastic wrap, then roll it back and forth to form a log. (The dimensions of the log will be specified in the recipe.) Before chilling, wrap it securely in waxed paper or plastic wrap and seal the ends to prevent the dough from drying out, and to

prevent it from picking up other flavors or odors in the refrigerator. If your refrigerator shelves have ridges, place the rolls of dough in a pan so the dough won't get indentation marks from the shelves.

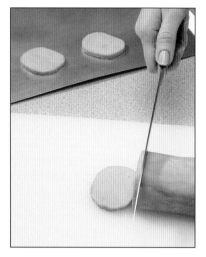

Chill the dough as long as the recipe requires. You'll know if the dough is firm enough as soon as you make the first cut—if it slices easily and cleanly, it is ready. Slice the dough with a sharp, thin-bladed knife to avoid tearing the dough. Use gentle pressure and a back-and-forth sawing motion when slicing the rolls so the cookies will keep their round shape. Rotating the dough a quarter-turn every four or five slices also helps keep logs of cookie dough round during slicing.

Bar Cookies

Bar cookies may be the easiest cookies to make—simply mix the batter, spread in a pan and bake. They are also quick to prepare since they bake all at once rather than in batches on a cookie sheet. The dough should be pressed or spread evenly in the pan before baking; use a spatula to push the dough out to the sides and into the corners so the bars will have an even thickness. If the dough is very thick, it may be easier to spread it with your hands. (You may

need to dust your fingertips with flour or dampen your hands with water to prevent the dough from sticking.)

Always use the pan size called for in the recipe. Substituting a different pan will affect the texture of your bar cookies: A smaller pan will result in thick and soggy bars; a larger pan will produce thinner bars with a drier texture. If you are using a dark nonstick pan or a glass baking dish instead of a standard shiny metal baking pan, reduce the oven temperature by 25°F. For easier cutting and cleanup, line the baking pan with foil. (See Preparing Pans, page 39.)

Most bar cookies should cool in the pan on a wire rack until barely warm or cool before cutting into bars or squares. (Some bar cookies are even easier to cut the next day.) Use a sharp knife with a thin blade, cutting straight down all the way through to the bottom of the pan; avoid using a sawing or back-and-forth motion. For very clean edges, wet the knife with hot water before cutting and wipe it with paper towels as needed. To make serving easy, remove a corner piece first, then remove the rest. Only cut as many bar cookies as you need at one time—with so many exposed surfaces, bar cookies tend to dry out quickly; they will remain fresher longer if they stay uncut in a covered pan.

Testing for Doneness

Most recipes provide two ways to help determine if cookies are done. The baking time is often given in a range, and cookies should be checked at the minimum baking time listed. A doneness test, such as looking at the color of the cookies or whether they are set, is typically more useful because every oven is different. Doneness tests vary with the type of cookie and the color of the dough. (Color descriptions are not very useful with darker doughs.) Watch cookies closely near the end of the baking time, because even one minute can be the difference between perfect and overbaked cookies.

Following are general guidelines that describe doneness tests for the basic types of cookies.

Drop Cookies: The surface is lightly browned and a slight imprint remains after touching the surface with your fingertip.

Hand-Formed Cookies: The edges are lightly browned.

Cutout Cookies: The edges are firm; the bottoms are lightly browned.

Refrigerator Cookies: The edges are firm; the bottoms are lightly browned.

Fudgelike Bar Cookies: The surface appears dull and a slight imprint remains after touching the surface with your fingertip.

Cakelike Bar Cookies: A wooden toothpick inserted into the center comes out clean and dry.

Cooling Cookies

Follow recipe directions for removing cookies from cookie sheets. Some thin refrigerator or cutout cookies should be removed from the cookie sheets immediately after baking. Most cookies, particularly larger ones, need to rest on the cookie sheets for 1 to 2 minutes to set; otherwise they may fall apart when being transferred to wire racks. However, if you leave cookies on a cookie sheet too long, they may stick and become difficult to remove without breaking them. If this happens, return the cookies to the oven for 1 to 2 minutes to warm them, then you should be able to remove them easily with a wide metal spatula.

Transferring cookies to wire racks to cool is essential, as it allows air to flow around the cookies and prevents them from becoming soggy. Bar cookies and brownies should be cooled in their pans on wire racks.

Decorating Cookies

Adding that special finishing touch to your cookies is easier than you might think. Melted chocolate, powdered sugar glaze, colored sugars and sprinkles are just a few of the simple decorations that can take cookies from simple to spectacular. Just be sure the cookies are completely cool before decorating them.

Chocolate for Dipping: Nothing makes a cookie stand out more than being partially or completely covered in chocolate. Just dip cookies in melted chocolate (semisweet, milk, white or some of each) and place them on a wire rack set over waxed paper until the chocolate is set. Adding a small amount of shortening to the chocolate when melting it (about one teaspoon for every four ounces of chocolate) is not necessary, but it will help keep the chocolate looking shiny after it sets.

Chocolate for Drizzling: For a quick decoration, use a fork or spoon to drizzle melted chocolate over cookies. For a more controlled drizzle, melt chocolate in a resealable plastic food storage bag and cut off a very tiny corner of the bag. Squeeze the melted chocolate in lines, squiggles, grids or patterns over cookies or bars. (A plastic squeeze bottle can also be used for this purpose.) If the chocolate glaze or melted chocolate is too thin, let it stand or refrigerate it until it thickens; if it is too thick, microwave it very briefly on Low (30% power).

Powdered Sugar Glaze or Icing: Blend one cup powdered sugar and five to six teaspoons water or milk to create a simple glaze that looks and tastes great on a variety of cookies. (Add additional sugar if the glaze is too thin; stir in a small amount of liquid if the glaze is too thick.) Powdered

sugar glaze can be used for drizzling and decorating like the melted chocolate described above, applied to cookies with a fork or spoon, plastic bag or squeeze bottle. This simple white glaze can be tinted with food coloring to add more excitement to cookies for special occasions; it can also be flavored with citrus juice, extracts or liqueur to complement the flavor of the cookies.

Powdered Sugar: A dusting of powdered sugar, sprinkled from a shaker or through a sifter or fine-meshed strainer, adds a beautiful touch to many cookies like thumbprints, crescents, rugelach, kolacky and lemon bars. For light-colored cookies, cocoa powder can also be used for dusting, or you can use half cocoa and half powdered sugar for a striking contrast.

For a fancier decoration, cut stencils out of cardboard or use a doily as a stencil. Place the stencil over the top of the cookie, dust with powdered sugar and carefully remove the stencil to see the design. (Always decorate with powdered sugar close to serving time, so it doesn't dissolve into the cookies and disappear.)

Prepared Toppings: Bottled ice cream toppings, such as fudge, caramel or butterscotch, can be used for a quick and easy decorative drizzle over cookies.

Colored Frostings: For simple and convenient decorating, small tubes of icing are available in the baking section of supermarkets. They are often packaged with several different tips so you can pipe dots, stars, lines, squiggles and other designs. These tubes tend to dry out quickly, so store them in a sealed plastic bag and use them within a few months after opening.

Fruit and Nuts: Dried and candied fruits add flavor and color to cookies—they can be pressed into cookies before they are baked or arranged on top of icing or glaze before it sets. Nuts can be used in similar fashion—whole, halved, chopped and sliced nuts can be pressed into cookies before baking, or used in combination with frosting or drizzle after the cookies are baked.

Colored Sugar and Sprinkles: Available in a dazzling array of colors, these decorations are primarily used on iced or frosted cookies, added when the icing is still moist. (They can also be pressed into rolls of refrigerator dough before baking.) Coarse-grained sugar, called crystal or decorating sugar, adds extra texture and sparkle to cookies.

Candies: Small colorful items such as red cinnamon candies, miniature marshmallows, jelly beans, nonpareils, gummy candies or chocolate-covered nuts or raisins are quick and easy decorations that can be pressed directly into cookies when they are still warm from the oven, or arranged on top of the icing before it sets.

Storing Cookies

- Cookies should be completely cool before storing them. Warm cookies produce steam, which will cause all the cookies in a container to become soggy.
- Line containers with waxed paper or aluminum foil (avoid plastic wrap). Whenever possible, use shallow containers for storing cookies. When you need to stack cookies, place sheets of waxed paper between the layers and don't stack more than three layers deep.
- Store soft and crisp cookies separately at room temperature to prevent changes in texture and flavor. It's best to store each variety of soft and crisp cookies in separate containers so they don't pick up flavors from other cookies.

  - Keep soft cookies in airtight containers or resealable plastic bags. If they begin to dry out, add a piece of apple or bread to the container to help retain moisture.
  - Store crisp cookies in containers with loose-fitting lids to prevent moisture build-up. If they become soggy, heat undecorated cookies in a 300°F oven for 3 to 5 minutes to restore crispness.
- Store cookies with sticky glazes, fragile decorations and icings in single layers between sheets of waxed paper. Make sure all frostings and decorations have set before storing the cookies.
- Sprinkle cookies with powdered sugar just before serving—if they are sprinkled earlier and stored, the sugar will be absorbed by the cookies and disappear.
- Bar cookies and brownies may be stored in their own baking pan, covered with aluminum foil or plastic wrap when cool. Most cookies and bars can be stored at room temperature for up to one week.

Freezing Cookies

- As a rule, crisp cookies freeze better than soft, moist cookies. Rich, buttery bar cookies and brownies are an exception to this rule since they freeze extremely well.
- It's best to freeze cookies that will be glazed or frosted in their undecorated state, as glazes often crack and discolor when frozen.
- Freeze cookies by type—never mix crisp cookies with soft cookies.
- Delicate cookies should be spread out on a cookie sheet (uncovered) and frozen solid before packing them in a container.
- Freeze baked cookies in sturdy airtight containers or in heavy-duty resealable freezer bags for up to six months. Place sheets of waxed paper between layers of cookies to prevent sticking. If the containers are not full, place a piece of

aluminum foil on top of the cookies to fill the empty space and protect the cookies from exposure to the air.

- Meringue-based cookies do not freeze well; they tend to absorb moisture and become soft.
- Sandwich cookies with jam, custard or cream fillings also do not freeze well; the individual cookies should be frozen and then filled later when the cookies are defrosted.
- Chocolate-dipped cookies will discolor if frozen. (Cookies garnished with chocolate should be decorated only after thawing).
- Most cookies and brownies should be thawed at room temperature, with the container opened slightly to allow the release of condensation. If you will be glazing, decorating or dusting the cookies with powdered sugar, be sure they are completely thawed first.
- Cookies that have been frozen can be refreshed in a 325°F oven to revive some of their fresh-baked flavor. Spread the cookies on a cookie sheet and heat for 3 to 8 minutes. (Small, thin cookies require less time to reheat, while large, thick cookies will take a little more time.) When you begin to notice a delicious aroma coming from the oven, the cookies are ready. Serve frozen cookies as soon as possible after thawing, since they are not as moist as fresh-baked and tend to go stale more quickly.

Freezing Cookie Dough

Having frozen cookie dough on hand means you can always have fresh-baked cookies in minutes! Most unbaked cookie doughs can be frozen for up to six months, wrapped well in waxed paper or plastic wrap or in freezer bags or containers. You may want to form the cookie dough into rolls before freezing, so it can be easily sliced and baked as needed. Or, freeze individual mounds of cookie dough on cookie sheets, then place them in a resealable plastic freezer bag after they have frozen solid. If you will be not be baking many cookies at one time, freeze the dough in several smaller bags.

Whether you freeze the dough in containers, rolls or freezer bags, be sure to wrap it securely and press out all the air before sealing, then clearly label and date the packages. Frozen dough should be thawed in the refrigerator at least eight hours before baking. If it is still too stiff after this time, let the dough stand at room temperature until it is workable. There are a few types of dough that should not be frozen, including bar cookies that are made with batters (instead of thick doughs), meringue batter and macaroon batter.

Gift Wrapping Cookies

Homemade cookies are a thoughtful gift for any occasion. Simple cookies are made extraordinary when tucked into unique packages and lavished with decorative accessories. Keep in mind that if the container itself is not airtight, the entire package should be wrapped in a plastic bag so the cookies will not become stale.

Baskets & Boxes: These versatile hold-alls are available in a wide variety of materials and sizes. Large, sturdy ones are well-suited for packing entire gift themes.

Gift Bags: These handy totes come in many sizes and colors. Pack individual cookies in smaller bags; pack goodie-filled canisters or tins in larger bags.

Tins: Metal containers with tight-fitting lids are perfect for cookies. They also hold up well when sent through the mail.

Unique Containers: Many items not originally intended for storing cookies make wonderfully creative holders for home-baked treats, such as flowerpots and planters, hat boxes, baking dishes, mugs, bowls or toy pails.

Cellophane: Cellophane is an indispensable material for hard-to-wrap gifts such as plates of cookies. Gather the ends and secure them with a multitude of pretty ribbon.

Decorative Papers: Papers come in a variety of finishes, including glossy and metallic, and many can be enhanced with rubber stamps. Colorful tissue papers are perfect for tucking into gift boxes and bags.

Dishtowels and Napkins: Colorful kitchen towels and cloth napkins look beautiful when lining a basket of cookies or tied around the outside of a container.

Gift Tags: Assorted metal and paper tags come in handy when making personalized notes and cards for your gifts. They also make great labels for storing directions, serving suggestions or even your recipe.

Raffia: Tuck assorted colors of raffia into boxes, baskets and pails. Or, use it as ribbon and tie boxes and tins with rustic bows.

Ribbons, Satin Cords and Strings: Thick, colorful ribbons, metallic strings and thin shiny cords add a touch of glamour to any kind of wrapping paper.

Rubber Stamps: Stamps with holiday or food themes paired with colorful inks are perfect for decorating plain papers or wrapping and making personalized note cards for recipes, storing directions and gift tags.

Little Extras: Make your gift even more appealing by attaching a cookie cutter, wooden spoon, whisk or spice jar to the package.

Shipping and Mailing Cookies

When you can't be with the ones you love, bake them some cookies! Keep the following tips in mind when shipping those special treats.

- Prepare soft, moist cookies that can handle jostling, rather than fragile, brittle cookies that might crumble. Most drop cookies, refrigerated cookies, shortbread and biscotti are good candidates for shipping; thin or tender cookies, sandwich cookies, frosted cookies and meringues are not.
- Brownies and bar cookies are generally sturdy, although it is best to avoid shipping any with moist fillings and frostings, since they become sticky at room temperature. For the same reason, shipping anything with chocolate during the summer, or to warm climates, is also risky.
- Wrap each type of cookie separately to retain flavors and textures. Cookies can also be wrapped back-to-back in pairs with either plastic wrap or foil.

- Bar cookies should be packed in layers the size of the container, or they can be sent in a covered foil pan, as long as the pan is well-cushioned inside the shipping box.
- Place wrapped cookies as tightly as possible in snug rows inside a sturdy shipping box or container.
- Fill the bottom of the shipping container with an even layer of packing material such as bubble wrap, styrofoam peanuts, shredded paper or crumpled newspaper. Do not use popped popcorn or puffed cereal, as it may attract insects. Place crumpled waxed paper, newspaper or paper towels in between layers of wrapped cookies. Fill any crevices with packing material, and add a final layer at the top of the box. Leaving no empty spaces in the container prevents the cookies from moving around.
- Ship the container to arrive as soon as possible, via overnight mail or another shipper that will deliver within a few days. Plainly mark "FRAGILE" in large letters on all sides of the package to encourage careful handling.

troubleshooting

Cookies are generally easy to make, but lots of little variables—inaccurate measurements, oven hot spots, even weather conditions—can cause them to turn out less than perfect. Knowing what the problems are and how to solve them can make your cookie baking experiences more enjoyable.

Problem: The dough is too soft.

Solution: Chill the dough until it is firm enough to handle or add an additional tablespoon or two of flour.

Problem: The dough is very crumbly and cracks when it is rolled.

Solution: If the dough feels too cold, let it stand at room temperature until it is workable. Or add a tablespoon or two of liquid (milk, cream or water) to the dough.

Problem: The cookies spread too much.

Solution: Make sure the butter you use in the dough is not too soft or partially melted. Chill the dough briefly and keep the dough refrigerated between batches of cookies. Avoid placing the dough on hot cookie sheets. As a last resort, add two to three tablespoons of flour to the dough, then bake several test cookies to see if the cookies have the right texture.

Problem: The cookies bake unevenly.

Solution: For drop or hand-formed cookies, the dough should be a uniform size and shape; for cutout cookies, the dough must be rolled out to an even thickness. To compensate for oven hot spots, rotate the cookie sheets from top to bottom and front to back during baking.

Problem: The cookies are too dry, dark and/or crisp.

Solution: Use an oven thermometer to check the accuracy of your oven temperature, as dry cookies are commonly the result of overbaking—your oven might be significantly hotter than the reading on the dial. Very thin or dark cookie sheets can cause dark cookies (reduce the oven temperature by 25°F if using dark sheets), as can baking the cookies too close to the top or bottom of the oven. Too much flour is also the culprit in many extra-crisp cookies; the flour must be measured accurately and not packed into the measuring cup.

Problem: The cookies break apart when transferring them to a cooling rack.

Solution: Let the cookies stand several minutes on the cookie sheet to set before moving them.

Problem: The cookies stick to the cookie sheet.

Solution: Try greasing the cookie sheets a little more, or try parchment paper instead—its nonstick surface releases even the most problematic cookies. If cookies are sticking after resting too long on the cookie sheets, return them to the oven for 1 to 2 minutes and then transfer the cookies to wire racks immediately.

Problem: The bar cookies are dry and hard.

Solution: Check the pan size to make sure it is exactly what was called for in the recipe—a pan too large will cause bars and brownies to be dry. Overly dry bar cookies can also be the result of too much flour, an oven that is too hot or using a dark nonstick pan or glass baking dish without reducing the oven temperature by 25°F.

bakers' substitutions

For the best results, always use the exact ingredients listed in a recipe. But if you have to substitute, try the following suggestions.

If you don't have:	Use:
1 cup cake flour	1 cup minus 2 tablespoons all-purpose flour
1 cup firmly packed brown sugar	1 cup granulated sugar mixed with 2 tablespoons molasses
1 teaspoon baking powder	¼ teaspoon baking soda plus ½ teaspoon cream of tartar
1 cup whole milk	1 cup skim milk plus 2 tablespoons melted butter
1 cup buttermilk	1 tablespoon lemon juice or vinegar plus milk to equal 1 cup (Stir; let mixture stand 5 minutes.)
1 cup sour cream	1 cup plain yogurt
1 cup honey	1¼ cups granulated sugar plus ¼ cup water
1 cup molasses	1 cup dark corn syrup or honey
½ cup corn syrup	½ cup granulated sugar plus 2 tablespoons liquid
½ cup raisins	½ cup currants, dried cranberries, chopped dates or chopped prunes
1 ounce (1 square) unsweetened chocolate	3 tablespoons unsweetened cocoa plus 1 tablespoon shortening
1 ounce (1 square) semisweet chocolate	1 ounce unsweetened chocolate plus 1 tablespoon sugar
1 cup semisweet chocolate chips	6 ounces semisweet baking chocolate, chopped
1 teaspoon fresh grated lemon peel	½ teaspoon dried lemon peel
1 teaspoon pumpkin pie spice	Combine ½ teaspoon ground cinnamon, ¼ teaspoon ground ginger, ⅛ teaspoon ground allspice and ⅛ teaspoon ground nutmeg

drop cookies

Island Cookies

1⅔ cups all-purpose flour
¾ teaspoon baking powder
½ teaspoon baking soda
½ teaspoon salt
¾ cup (1½ sticks) butter, softened
¾ cup packed brown sugar
⅓ cup granulated sugar
1 teaspoon vanilla extract
1 large egg
1¾ cups (11.5-ounce package) NESTLÉ® TOLL HOUSE®
    Milk Chocolate Morsels
1 cup flaked coconut, toasted, if desired
1 cup chopped walnuts

PREHEAT oven to 375°F.

COMBINE flour, baking powder, baking soda and salt in small bowl. Beat butter, brown sugar, granulated sugar and vanilla extract in large mixer bowl until creamy. Beat in egg. Gradually beat in flour mixture. Stir in morsels, coconut and nuts. Drop by slightly rounded tablespoon onto ungreased baking sheets.

BAKE for 8 to 11 minutes or until edges are lightly browned. Cool on baking sheets for 2 minutes; remove to wire racks to cool completely.

Makes about 3 dozen cookies

Note: NESTLÉ® TOLL HOUSE® Semi-Sweet Chocolate Morsels, Semi-Sweet Chocolate Mini Morsels, Premier White Morsels or Butterscotch Flavored Morsels may be substituted for the Milk Chocolate Morsels.

Island Cookies

Double Chocolate Cranberry Chunkies

1¾ cups all-purpose flour
⅓ cup unsweetened cocoa powder
½ teaspoon baking powder
½ teaspoon salt
1 cup (2 sticks) butter, softened
1 cup granulated sugar
½ cup packed brown sugar
1 egg
1 teaspoon vanilla
2 cups semisweet chocolate chunks or large chocolate chips
¾ cup dried cranberries or dried tart cherries
Additional granulated sugar

1. Preheat oven to 350°F.

2. Combine flour, cocoa, baking powder and salt in small bowl; set aside. Beat butter, 1 cup granulated sugar and brown sugar in large bowl with electric mixer at medium speed until light and fluffy. Beat in egg and vanilla until well blended. Gradually beat in flour mixture on low speed until blended. Stir in chocolate chunks and cranberries.

3. Drop dough by level ¼ cupfuls onto ungreased cookie sheets, spacing 3 inches apart. Flatten dough until 2 inches in diameter with bottom of glass that has been dipped in additional granulated sugar.

4. Bake 11 to 12 minutes or until cookies are set. Cool cookies 2 minutes on cookie sheets; transfer to wire racks. Cool completely.

Makes about 1 dozen (4-inch) cookies

Double Chocolate Cranberry Chunkies

Pineapple and White Chip Drops

　1 cup (2 sticks) butter or margarine, softened
　1 cup sugar
　2 eggs
　½ teaspoon vanilla extract
　1 can (8 ounces) crushed pineapple, with juice
3½ cups all-purpose flour
　1 teaspoon baking soda
　¾ teaspoon ground cinnamon
　½ teaspoon salt
　¼ teaspoon ground nutmeg
　1 cup chopped pecans
1⅔ cups (10-ounce package) HERSHEY'S Premier White Chips

1. Heat oven to 350°F. Lightly grease cookie sheet.

2. Beat butter and sugar in large bowl until well blended. Add eggs and vanilla; blend well. Blend in pineapple and juice. Stir together flour, baking soda, cinnamon, salt and nutmeg; gradually add to butter mixture, beating until well blended. Stir in pecans and white chips. Drop by tablespoons onto prepared cookie sheet.

3. Bake 10 to 12 minutes or until lightly browned around edges. Remove from cookie sheet to wire rack. Cool completely.　　　*Makes about 5 dozen cookies*

Pineapple and White Chip Drops

Milk Chocolate Florentine Cookies

⅔ **cup butter**
2 **cups quick oats**
1 **cup granulated sugar**
⅔ **cup all-purpose flour**
¼ **cup light or dark corn syrup**
¼ **cup milk**
1 **teaspoon vanilla extract**
¼ **teaspoon salt**
1¾ **cups (11.5-ounce package) NESTLÉ® TOLL HOUSE®**
Milk Chocolate Morsels

PREHEAT oven to 375°F. Line baking sheets with foil.

MELT butter in medium saucepan; remove from heat. Stir in oats, sugar, flour, corn syrup, milk, vanilla extract and salt; mix well. Drop by level teaspoon, about 3 inches apart, onto prepared baking sheets. Spread thinly with rubber spatula.

BAKE for 6 to 8 minutes or until golden brown. Cool completely on baking sheets on wire racks. Peel foil from cookies.

MICROWAVE morsels in medium, uncovered microwave-safe bowl on MEDIUM-HIGH (70%) power for 1 minute. STIR. Morsels may retain some of their original shape. If necessary, microwave at additional 10- to 15-second intervals, stirring just until morsels are melted. Spread thin layer of melted chocolate onto flat side of *half* the cookies. Top with *remaining* cookies.

Makes about 3½ dozen sandwich cookies

Milk Chocolate Florentine Cookies

Quebec Maple-Pecan Drops

Cookies
- ½ **cup (1 stick) butter, softened**
- ½ **cup granulated sugar**
- 3 **tablespoons maple-flavored syrup**
- 1 **cup all-purpose flour**
- ½ **teaspoon baking soda**
- ¼ **teaspoon salt**
- 1 **cup uncooked quick oats (not old-fashioned oats)**
- ½ **cup coarsely chopped pecans, toasted**
- ¼ **cup packaged chopped pitted dates**

Frosting (optional)
- 2 **ounces cream cheese, softened**
- 2 **tablespoons butter, softened**
- 2 **tablespoons maple-flavored syrup**
- 1½ **cups sifted powdered sugar**
- ⅓ **cup finely chopped pecans, toasted**

1. For cookies, preheat oven to 350°F. Beat ½ cup butter and granulated sugar in large bowl with electric mixer at medium speed until creamy. Beat in 3 tablespoons syrup. Combine flour, baking soda and salt; gradually beat into butter mixture. On low speed, beat in oats, coarsely chopped pecans and dates.

2. Drop dough by rounded tablespoonfuls 2 inches apart onto ungreased cookie sheets. Bake 12 minutes or until cookies are golden brown. Let stand on cookie sheets 2 minutes; transfer to wire racks and cool completely.

3. For frosting, beat cream cheese and 2 tablespoons butter in small bowl with electric mixer at medium speed until smooth. Beat in 2 tablespoons syrup. Gradually beat in powdered sugar until smooth. Spread frosting over cooled cookies; top with finely chopped pecans. *Makes about 2 dozen cookies*

Quebec Maple-Pecan Drops

Mocha Latte Thins

⅓ cup all-purpose flour
⅛ teaspoon salt
¾ cup sugar
½ cup (1 stick) plus 1 tablespoon unsalted butter, softened, divided
  2 eggs
1½ teaspoons vanilla
  2 tablespoons instant espresso powder, dissolved in 2 tablespoons
    hot water
  3 (3½-ounce) bars bittersweet chocolate, finely chopped
¼ cup white chocolate chips

1. Sift together flour and salt; set aside. Beat sugar and ½ cup butter until creamy. Add eggs and vanilla; beat until smooth. Stir in espresso mixture. (There will be some extra grounds that will not dissolve. Do not stir in.)

2. Add flour mixture to butter mixture; beat just until blended. Fold in chocolate. Refrigerate dough at least 2 hours or overnight.

3. Preheat oven to 350°F. Line cookie sheets with parchment paper; grease paper. Drop by level teaspoonfuls about 1 inch apart, 20 to a pan. (Dough will still be sticky and may require some molding with fingers.) Bake 7 to 8 minutes or until lightly browned.

4. Let cookies cool on cookie sheets 1 minute. Transfer to wire racks; cool completely.

5. Combine white chocolate chips and remaining 1 tablespoon butter in microwavable bowl. Microwave at HIGH (100%) 50 seconds; stir well. If necessary, microwave at additional 10-second intervals until chocolate is completely melted when stirred. Drizzle from tip of spoon onto cooled cookies. *Makes about 8 dozen thins*

Note: Cookies are very crisp when first baked. They become softer after a few hours. Store in tightly covered container.

Mocha Latte Thins

Original Nestlé® Toll House® Chocolate Chip Cookies

2¼ cups all-purpose flour
1 teaspoon baking soda
1 teaspoon salt
1 cup (2 sticks) butter or margarine, softened
¾ cup granulated sugar
¾ cup packed brown sugar
1 teaspoon vanilla extract
2 large eggs
2 cups (12-ounce package) NESTLÉ® TOLL HOUSE®
    Semi-Sweet Chocolate Morsels
1 cup chopped nuts

PREHEAT oven to 375°F.

COMBINE flour, baking soda and salt in small bowl. Beat butter, granulated sugar, brown sugar and vanilla extract in large mixer bowl until creamy. Add eggs, one at a time, beating well after each addition. Gradually beat in flour mixture. Stir in morsels and nuts. Drop by rounded tablespoon onto ungreased baking sheets.

BAKE for 9 to 11 minutes or until golden brown. Cool on baking sheets for 2 minutes; remove to wire racks to cool completely.

Makes about 5 dozen cookies

Pan Cookie Variation: GREASE 15×10-inch jelly-roll pan. Prepare dough as above. Spread into prepared pan. Bake for 20 to 25 minutes or until golden brown. Cool in pan on wire rack. Makes 4 dozen bars.

Slice and Bake Cookie Variation: PREPARE dough as above. Divide in half; wrap in wax paper. Refrigerate for 1 hour or until firm. Shape each half into 15-inch log; wrap in wax paper. Refrigerate for 30 minutes.* Preheat oven to 375°F. Cut into ½-inch-thick slices; place on ungreased baking sheets. Bake for 8 to 10 minutes or until golden brown. Cool on baking sheets for 2 minutes; remove to wire racks to cool completely. Makes about 5 dozen cookies.

*Dough may be stored in refrigerator for up to 1 week or in freezer for up to 8 weeks.

Original Nestlé® Toll House® Chocolate Chip Cookies

Crispy Oat Drops

1 cup (2 sticks) butter or margarine, softened
½ cup granulated sugar
½ cup firmly packed light brown sugar
1 large egg
2 cups all-purpose flour
½ cup quick-cooking or old-fashioned oats, uncooked
1 teaspoon cream of tartar
½ teaspoon baking soda
¼ teaspoon salt
1¾ cups "M&M's"® Semi-Sweet Chocolate Mini Baking Bits
1 cup toasted rice cereal
½ cup shredded coconut
½ cup coarsely chopped pecans

Preheat oven to 350°F. In large bowl cream butter and sugars until light and fluffy; beat in egg. In medium bowl combine flour, oats, cream of tartar, baking soda and salt; blend flour mixture into creamed mixture. Stir in "M&M's"® Semi-Sweet Chocolate Mini Baking Bits, cereal, coconut and pecans. Drop by heaping tablespoonfuls about 2 inches apart onto ungreased cookie sheets. Bake 10 to 13 minutes or until lightly browned. Cool completely on wire racks. Store in tightly covered container.

Makes about 4 dozen cookies

Crispy Oat Drops

Pumpkin Spiced and Iced Cookies

2¼ cups all-purpose flour
1½ teaspoons pumpkin pie spice
  1 teaspoon baking powder
  ½ teaspoon baking soda
  ½ teaspoon salt
  1 cup (2 sticks) butter or margarine, softened
  1 cup granulated sugar
  1 can (15 ounces) LIBBY'S® 100% Pure Pumpkin
  2 large eggs
  1 teaspoon vanilla extract
  2 cups (12-ounce package) NESTLÉ® TOLL HOUSE®
    Semi-Sweet Chocolate Morsels
  1 cup chopped walnuts (optional)
  Vanilla Glaze (recipe follows)

PREHEAT oven to 375°F. Grease baking sheets.

COMBINE flour, pumpkin pie spice, baking powder, baking soda and salt in medium bowl. Beat butter and granulated sugar in large mixer bowl until creamy. Beat in pumpkin, eggs and vanilla extract. Gradually beat in flour mixture. Stir in morsels and nuts. Drop by rounded tablespoon onto prepared baking sheets.

BAKE for 15 to 20 minutes or until edges are lightly browned. Cool on baking sheets for 2 minutes; remove to wire rack to cool completely. Spread or drizzle with Vanilla Glaze. *Makes about 5½ dozen cookies*

Vanilla Glaze: COMBINE 1 cup powdered sugar, 1 to 1½ tablespoons milk and ½ teaspoon vanilla extract in small bowl; mix well.

Pumpkin Spiced and Iced Cookies

Breakfast Cookies

**1 Butter Flavor CRISCO® Stick or 1 cup Butter Flavor CRISCO®
all-vegetable shortening**
1 cup JIF® Extra Crunchy Peanut Butter
¾ cup granulated sugar
¾ cup firmly packed brown sugar
2 eggs, beaten
1½ cups all-purpose flour
1 teaspoon baking powder
1 teaspoon baking soda
1 teaspoon ground cinnamon
1¾ cups quick oats, uncooked
1¼ cups raisins
1 medium Granny Smith apple, finely grated, including juice
⅓ cup finely grated carrot
¼ cup flake coconut (optional)

Preheat oven to 350°F. Place sheets of foil on countertop for cooling cookies.

Combine 1 cup shortening, peanut butter and sugars in large bowl. Beat at medium speed with electric mixer until blended. Beat in eggs.

Combine flour, baking powder, baking soda and cinnamon. Add gradually to creamed mixture at low speed. Beat until blended. Sir in oats, raisins, apple, carrot and coconut. Drop by tablespoonfuls onto ungreased baking sheet.

Bake for 9 to 11 minutes or until just browned around edges. Do not overbake. Cool 2 minutes on baking sheet. Remove cookies to foil to cool completely.
Makes 5 to 6 dozen cookies

Tip: Freeze cookies between sheets of waxed paper in sealed container. Use as needed for breakfast on-the-run or as a nutritious snack.

Breakfast Cookies

Hungarian Lemon Poppy Seed Cookies

Cookies
   ⅔ cup granulated sugar
   ½ cup (1 stick) butter, softened
   1 egg
   2 teaspoons grated lemon peel
1¼ cups all-purpose flour
   ½ teaspoon baking soda
   ¼ teaspoon salt
   1 tablespoon poppy seeds

Glaze
   1 cup powdered sugar
   2 tablespoons lemon juice

1. Preheat oven to 350°F.

2. For cookies, beat granulated sugar and butter in large bowl with electric mixer at medium speed until creamy. Beat in egg and lemon peel. Combine flour, baking soda and salt; gradually add to butter mixture. Beat in poppy seeds on low speed.

3. Drop dough by heaping teaspoonfuls 2 inches apart onto ungreased cookie sheets. Bake 11 to 12 minutes or until edges are lightly browned. Let stand on cookie sheets 1 minute; transfer to wire racks and cool completely.

4. For glaze, combine powdered sugar and lemon juice in small bowl; mix well. Drizzle glaze over cookies; let stand until glaze is set, about 20 minutes.

Makes about 2 dozen cookies

Hungarian Lemon Poppy Seed Cookies

Chocolate Cherry Treats

½ cup (1 stick) butter, softened
¾ cup firmly packed light brown sugar
¼ cup granulated sugar
½ cup sour cream
1 large egg
1 tablespoon maraschino cherry juice
1 teaspoon vanilla extract
2 cups all-purpose flour
½ teaspoon baking soda
¼ teaspoon salt
1¼ cups "M&M's"® Milk Chocolate Mini Baking Bits
½ cup chopped walnuts
⅓ cup well-drained chopped maraschino cherries

Preheat oven to 350°F. In large bowl cream butter and sugars until light and fluffy; beat in sour cream, egg, maraschino cherry juice and vanilla. In medium bowl combine flour, baking soda and salt; add to creamed mixture. Stir in "M&M's"® Milk Chocolate Mini Baking Bits, walnuts and maraschino cherries. Drop by heaping tablespoonfuls about 2 inches apart onto ungreased cookie sheets. Bake about 15 minutes. Cool 1 minute on cookie sheets; cool completely on wire racks. Store in tightly covered container.   *Makes 3 dozen cookies*

Chocolate Cherry Treats

Baker's® Premium Chocolate Chunk Cookies

1¾ cups flour
¾ teaspoon baking soda
¼ teaspoon salt
¾ cup (1½ sticks) butter or margarine, softened
½ cup granulated sugar
½ cup firmly packed brown sugar
1 egg
1 teaspoon vanilla
1 package (12 ounces) BAKER'S® Semi-Sweet Chocolate Chunks
1 cup chopped PLANTERS® Walnuts or Pecans

MIX flour, baking soda and salt in medium bowl; set aside.

BEAT butter and sugars in large bowl with electric mixer on medium speed until light and fluffy. Add egg and vanilla; beat well. Gradually beat in flour mixture. Stir in chocolate chunks and walnuts. Drop by heaping tablespoonfuls onto ungreased cookie sheets.

BAKE at 375°F for 11 to 13 minutes or just until golden brown. Cool on cookie sheets 1 minute. Remove to wire racks and cool completely.

Makes about 3 dozen cookies

Variation: Spread dough in greased foil-lined 15×10×1-inch baking pan. Bake at 375°F for 18 to 20 minutes or until golden brown. (Or, bake in 13×9-inch pan for 20 to 22 minutes.) Cool completely in pan on wire rack.

Chocolate Chunkoholic Cookies: Omit nuts. Stir in 2 packages (12 ounces each) BAKER'S® Semi-Sweet Chocolate Chunks. Drop by scant ¼ cupfuls onto cookie sheets. Bake at 375°F for 12 to 14 minutes. Makes about 22 large cookies.

Freezing Cookie Dough: Freeze heaping tablespoonfuls of cookie dough on cookie sheet 1 hour. Transfer to airtight plastic container or freezer zipper-style plastic bag. Freeze dough up to 1 month. Bake frozen cookie dough on ungreased cookie sheets at 375°F for 15 to 16 minutes or just until golden brown.

Prep Time: 15 minutes
Bake Time: 28 minutes

Baker's® Premium Chocolate Chunk Cookies

Applesauce Raisin Chews

1 cup (2 sticks) margarine or butter, softened
1 cup firmly packed brown sugar
1 cup applesauce
1 egg
1 teaspoon vanilla
2 cups all-purpose flour
1 teaspoon baking soda
1 teaspoon ground cinnamon
½ teaspoon salt (optional)
2½ cups QUAKER® Oats (quick or old fashioned, uncooked)
1 cup raisins

Heat oven to 350°F. Beat together margarine and sugar until creamy. Add applesauce, egg and vanilla; beat well. Add combined flour, baking soda, cinnamon and salt; mix well. Stir in oats and raisins. Drop by rounded tablespoonfuls onto ungreased cookie sheets. Bake 11 to 13 minutes or until light golden brown. Cool 1 minute on cookie sheets; remove to wire racks. Cool completely. Store in tightly covered container.

Makes about 4 dozen

Mini Morsel Meringue Cookies

4 large egg whites
½ teaspoon salt
½ teaspoon cream of tartar
1 cup granulated sugar
2 cups (12-ounce package) NESTLÉ® TOLL HOUSE®
    Semi-Sweet Chocolate Mini Morsels

PREHEAT oven to 300°F. Grease baking sheets.

BEAT egg whites, salt and cream of tartar in small mixer bowl until soft peaks form. Gradually add sugar; beat until stiff peaks form. Gently fold in morsels ⅓ cup at a time. Drop by level tablespoon onto prepared baking sheets.

BAKE for 20 to 25 minutes or until meringues are dry and crisp. Cool on baking sheets for 2 minutes; remove to wire racks to cool completely. Store in airtight containers.

Makes about 5 dozen cookies

Fresh Orange Cookies

   1½ **cups all-purpose flour**
   ½ **teaspoon baking soda**
   ¼ **teaspoon salt**
   ½ **cup butter or margarine, softened**
   ½ **cup granulated sugar**
   ½ **cup packed light brown sugar**
   1 **egg**
   1 **unpeeled SUNKIST® orange, finely chopped***
   ½ **cup chopped walnuts**
     Orange Glaze (recipe follows)

Chop SUNKIST® orange in blender or food processor, or by hand, to equal ¾ cup chopped fruit.

Sift together flour, baking soda and salt. In large bowl, beat butter and sugars until light and fluffy. Add egg and chopped orange; beat well. Gradually blend in dry ingredients. Stir in walnuts. Cover and chill at least 1 hour. Drop dough by teaspoons onto lightly greased cookie sheets. Bake at 375°F for 10 to 12 minutes. Cool on wire racks. Spread cookies with Orange Glaze.   *Makes about 4 dozen cookies*

Orange Glaze

   1 **cup confectioners' sugar**
   1 **to 2 tablespoons fresh SUNKIST® orange juice**
   1 **tablespoon butter or margarine, softened**
   1 **teaspoon grated SUNKIST® orange peel**

In small bowl, combine all ingredients until smooth.   *Makes about ½ cup*

Oatmeal Toffee Cookies

1 cup (2 sticks) butter or margarine, softened
2 cups packed light brown sugar
2 eggs
2 teaspoons vanilla extract
1¾ cups all-purpose flour
1 teaspoon baking soda
1 teaspoon ground cinnamon
½ teaspoon salt
3 cups quick-cooking oats
1¾ cups (10-ounce package) HEATH® BITS 'O BRICKLE Almond Toffee Bits or SKOR® English Toffee Bits
1 cup MOUNDS® Sweetened Coconut Flakes (optional)

1. Heat oven to 375°F. Lightly grease cookie sheet. Beat butter, brown sugar, eggs and vanilla until well blended. Add flour, baking soda, cinnamon and salt; beat until blended.

2. Stir in oats, toffee and coconut, if desired, with spoon. Drop dough by rounded teaspoons about 2 inches apart onto prepared sheet.

3. Bake 8 to 10 minutes or until edges are lightly browned. Cool 1 minute; remove to wire rack. *Makes about 4 dozen cookies*

Oatmeal Toffee Cookies

Tropical Chunk Cookies

    1 package (12 ounces) BAKER'S® White Chocolate Chunks, divided
1¾ cups flour
1½ cups BAKER'S® ANGEL FLAKE® Coconut, toasted
  ¾ teaspoon baking soda
  ¼ teaspoon salt
  ½ cup (1 stick) butter or margarine, softened
  ⅓ cup firmly packed brown sugar
  1 egg
  1 teaspoon vanilla
  1 cup chopped PLANTERS® Macadamias

MICROWAVE 1 cup of the chocolate chunks in microwavable bowl on HIGH 2 minutes until almost melted. Stir until chocolate is completely melted; cool slightly. Mix flour, coconut, baking soda and salt in medium bowl; set aside.

BEAT butter and sugar in large bowl with electric mixer on medium speed until light and fluffy. Add egg and vanilla; beat well. Stir in melted chocolate. Gradually add flour mixture, mixing until well blended. Stir in remaining chocolate chunks and nuts. Drop by heaping tablespoonfuls onto ungreased cookie sheets.

BAKE 375°F for 11 to 13 minutes or just until golden brown. Cool on cookie sheets 1 minute. Cool completely on wire rack.   *Makes about 3 dozen cookies*

How to Toast Coconut: Spread coconut in single layer on cookie sheet. Bake at 350°F for 7 to 8 minutes or until lightly browned, stirring frequently.

Prep Time: 15 minutes
Bake Time: 13 minutes

Tropical Chunk Cookies

hand-formed cookies

Peanut Butter Kisses

1 cup granulated sugar
1 cup packed brown sugar
1 cup CRISCO® all-vegetable shortening
1 cup JIF® Peanut Butter
2 eggs
¼ cup milk
2 teaspoons vanilla
3½ cups sifted all-purpose flour
2 teaspoons baking soda
1 teaspoon salt
1 (11-ounce) package milk chocolate candies

Preheat oven to 375°F.

Cream together granulated sugar, brown sugar, 1 cup shortening and peanut butter. Add eggs, milk and vanilla; beat well.

Stir together flour, baking soda and salt; add to peanut butter mixture. Beat well. Shape into 1-inch balls; roll in additional granulated sugar. Place on ungreased cookie sheet.

Bake for 8 minutes. Remove from oven. Press one milk chocolate candy into center of each warm cookie. Return to oven; bake 3 minutes longer.

Makes 6 to 7 dozen cookies

Peanut Butter Kisses

Sensational Cinnamon Chip Biscotti

½ cup (1 stick) butter, softened
1 cup sugar
2 eggs
1 teaspoon vanilla extract
2½ cups all-purpose flour
1½ teaspoons baking powder
¼ teaspoon salt
1⅔ cups (10-ounce package) HERSHEY'S Cinnamon Chips, divided
1 cup very finely chopped walnuts
2 teaspoons shortening (do not use butter, margarine, spread or oil)
White Chip Drizzle (recipe follows)

1. Heat oven 325°F. Lightly grease cookie sheet.

2. Beat butter and sugar in large bowl until blended. Add eggs and vanilla; beat well. Stir together flour, baking powder and salt; gradually add to butter mixture, beating until smooth. (Dough will be stiff.) Using spoon or with hands, work 1 cup cinnamon chips and walnuts into dough.

3. Divide dough into four equal parts. Shape each part into log about 8 inches long. Place on prepared cookie sheet at least 2 inches apart; flatten slightly.

4. Bake 25 to 30 minutes or until logs are set and wooden pick inserted in center comes out clean. Remove from oven; let cool on cookie sheet 30 minutes. Transfer to cutting board. Using serrated knife and sawing motion, cut logs diagonally into ½-inch-wide slices. Place slices close together, cut side down, on ungreased cookie sheet. Return to oven; bake 5 to 6 minutes. Turn each slice; bake an additional 5 to 8 minutes. Remove from oven; cool slightly. Remove from cookie sheet to wire rack; cool completely. Melt remaining cinnamon chips with shortening; drizzle over each cookie. Drizzle White Chip Drizzle over top.   *Makes about 5 dozen cookies*

White Chip Drizzle: Place ¼ cup HERSHEY'S Premier White Chips and 1 teaspoon shortening (do not use butter, margarine, spread or oil) in small microwave-safe bowl. Microwave at HIGH (100%) 30 to 45 seconds or until smooth when stirred.

Sensational Cinnamon Chip Biscotti

Chocolate-Gilded Danish Sugar Cones

½ cup (1 stick) butter, softened
½ cup sugar
½ cup all-purpose flour
2 egg whites
1 teaspoon vanilla
3 ounces bittersweet chocolate *or* ½ cup semisweet chocolate chips

1. Preheat oven to 400°F. Generously grease 4 cookie sheets. Beat butter and sugar in large bowl until light and fluffy. Blend in flour. In clean, dry bowl, beat egg whites until foamy. Blend into butter mixture. Add vanilla. Using teaspoon, place 4 mounds of dough 4 inches apart on each prepared cookie sheet. Spread mounds to 3-inch diameter with small spatula dipped in water.

2. Bake 1 sheet at a time, 5 to 6 minutes or until edges are just barely golden. (Do not overbake, or cookies will become crisp too quickly and will be difficult to shape.) Remove from oven and quickly loosen each cookie from cookie sheet with thin spatula. Shape each cookie into cone. Cones will become firm as they cool. (If cookies become too firm to shape, return to oven for few seconds to soften.)

3. Melt chocolate in small bowl over hot water. Stir until smooth. When all cookies are baked and cooled, dip wide ends into melted chocolate; let stand until chocolate is set.
Makes about 16 cookies

Chocolate-Gilded Danish Sugar Cones

Mini Chip Snowball Cookies

1½ cups (3 sticks) butter or margarine, softened
¾ cup powdered sugar
1 tablespoon vanilla extract
½ teaspoon salt
3 cups all-purpose flour
2 cups (12-ounce package) NESTLÉ® TOLL HOUSE®
    Semi-Sweet Chocolate Mini Morsels
½ cup finely chopped nuts
    Powdered sugar

PREHEAT oven to 375°F.

BEAT butter, sugar, vanilla extract and salt in large mixer bowl until creamy. Gradually beat in flour; stir in morsels and nuts. Shape level tablespoons of dough into 1¼-inch balls. Place on ungreased baking sheets.

BAKE for 10 to 12 minutes or until cookies are set and lightly browned. Remove from oven. Sift powdered sugar over hot cookies on baking sheets. Cool on baking sheets for 10 minutes; remove to wire racks to cool completely. Sprinkle with additional powdered sugar, if desired. Store in airtight containers.

Makes about 5 dozen cookies

Simpler Than Sin Peanut Chocolate Cookies

1 cup PETER PAN® Extra Crunchy Peanut Butter
1 cup sugar
1 egg, at room temperature and beaten
2 teaspoons vanilla
1 (6-ounce) dark or milk chocolate candy bar, broken into squares

Preheat oven to 350°F. In medium bowl, combine Peter Pan® Peanut Butter, sugar, egg and vanilla; mix well. Roll dough into 1-inch balls. Place 2 inches apart on ungreased cookie sheet. Bake 12 minutes. Remove from oven and place chocolate square in center of each cookie. Bake an additional 5 to 7 minutes or until cookies are lightly golden around edges. Cool 5 minutes. Remove to wire rack. Cool.

Makes 21 to 24 cookies

Note: This simple recipe is unusual because it doesn't contain any flour—but it still makes great cookies!

Mini Chip Snowball Cookies

Molded Scotch Shortbread

1½ cups all-purpose flour
¼ teaspoon salt
¾ cup (1½ sticks) butter, softened
⅓ cup sugar
1 egg

1. Preheat oven to temperature recommended by shortbread mold manufacturer. Spray 10-inch ceramic shortbread mold with nonstick cooking spray.

2. Combine flour and salt in medium bowl. Beat butter and sugar in large bowl with electric mixer at medium speed until light and fluffy. Beat in egg. Gradually add flour mixture. Beat at low speed until well blended.

3. Press dough firmly into mold. Bake, cool and remove from mold according to manufacturer's directions. *Makes 1 shortbread mold*

Note: If shortbread mold is not available, preheat oven to 350°F. Shape tablespoonfuls of dough into 1-inch balls. Place 2 inches apart on ungreased cookie sheets; press with fork to flatten. Bake 18 to 20 minutes or until edges are lightly browned. Let cookies stand on cookie sheets 2 minutes; transfer to wire racks to cool completely. Makes 2 dozen cookies.

Tip: Butter can be stored in the refrigerator up to 1 month. Be sure to wrap it airtight, as butter readily absorbs flavors and odors from other items in the refrigerator.

Molded Scotch Shortbread

Cocoa Ginger Crisps

1 cup (2 sticks) butter or margarine, softened
1⅓ cups sugar, divided
1 egg
¼ cup light corn syrup
2 cups all-purpose flour
6 tablespoons plus 1¼ teaspoons HERSHEY'S Cocoa, divided
2 teaspoons baking soda
¼ teaspoon ground ginger
¼ teaspoon salt

1. Beat butter, 1 cup sugar and egg in large bowl until fluffy. Add corn syrup; beat until well blended. Stir together flour, 6 tablespoons cocoa, baking soda, ginger and salt; gradually add to butter mixture, beating until well blended. Cover; refrigerate dough about 1 hour or until firm enough to handle.

2. Heat oven to 350°F.

3. Stir together remaining ⅓ cup sugar and 1¼ teaspoons cocoa in shallow bowl. Shape dough into 1-inch balls; roll in sugar-cocoa mixture to coat. Place about 2 inches apart on ungreased cookie sheet.

4. Bake 10 to 12 minutes or until cookies flatten. Cool 1 minute; remove from cookie sheet to wire rack. Cool completely. *Makes about 4 dozen cookies*

Cocoa Ginger Crisps

Classic Peanut Butter Cookies

  1 cup (2 sticks) unsalted butter, softened
  1 cup crunchy peanut butter
  1 cup granulated sugar
  1 cup light brown sugar, firmly packed
  2 eggs
  2½ cups all-purpose flour
  1½ teaspoons baking soda
  1 teaspoons baking powder
  ½ teaspoon salt

Beat butter, peanut butter and sugars until creamy. Beat in eggs. In separate bowl, sift flour, baking soda, baking powder and salt. Stir into batter until blended. Refrigerate 1 hour. Roll dough into 1-inch balls and place on baking sheets. Flatten each ball with fork, making criss-cross pattern. Bake in preheated 375°F oven about 10 minutes or until cookies begin to brown. Do not overbake.   *Makes 4 dozen cookies*

Favorite recipe from **Peanut Advisory Board**

Banana Crescents

  ½ cup chopped almonds, toasted
  6 tablespoons sugar, divided
  ½ cup margarine, cut into pieces
 1½ cups plus 2 tablespoons all-purpose flour
  ⅛ teaspoon salt
  1 extra-ripe, medium DOLE® Banana, peeled
  2 to 3 ounces semisweet chocolate chips

- Pulverize almonds with 2 tablespoons sugar in blender.

- Beat margarine, almond mixture, remaining 4 tablespoons sugar, flour and salt.

- Purée banana in blender; add to almond mixture and mix until well blended.

- Roll tablespoonfuls of dough into logs, then shape into crescents. Place on ungreased cookie sheet. Bake at 375°F 25 minutes or until golden. Cool on wire rack.

- Melt chocolate in microwavable dish at MEDIUM (50% power) 1½ to 2 minutes, stirring once. Dip ends of cookies in chocolate. Refrigerate until chocolate is set.
  Makes 2 dozen cookies

Chocolate Chunk Cranberry Biscotti

2 cups flour
1½ teaspoons CALUMET® Baking Powder
¼ teaspoon salt
½ cup (1 stick) butter or margarine, softened
½ cup sugar
2 eggs
1 teaspoon vanilla
1 package (12 ounces) BAKER'S® White Chocolate Chunks, divided
½ cup sweetened dried cranberries
½ cup chopped PLANTERS® Pecans (optional)

LIGHTLY grease and flour large cookie sheet. Mix flour, baking powder and salt in medium bowl; set aside.

BEAT butter and sugar in large bowl with electric mixer on medium speed until light and fluffy. Add eggs and vanilla; beat well. Gradually add flour mixture, mixing until well blended after each addition. Stir in 1½ cups of the chocolate chunks, cranberries and pecans.

DIVIDE dough in half. On floured board, shape each half into 14×1½-inch log. Place, 2 inches apart, on prepared cookie sheet.

BAKE at 325°F for 25 to 28 minutes or until lightly browned. Cool on cookie sheet 15 minutes. Place logs on cutting board; cut with serrated knife into ¾-inch-thick diagonal slices. Place cut sides down, ½ inch apart, on cookie sheet. Bake an additional 10 minutes or until slightly dry, turning over after 5 minutes. Remove to wire racks; cool completely.

MELT remaining chocolate chunks as directed on package. Drizzle over biscotti. Let stand until chocolate is firm. *Makes about 3 dozen cookies*

Storage Know-How: Store in tightly covered container up to 2 weeks.

Prep Time: 30 minutes
Total Time: 1 hour 40 minutes

Ma'moul (Date Pastries)

Filling
 1 pound chopped pitted dates
 ½ cup water
 ¼ cup granulated sugar
 1 teaspoon almond extract
 2 tablespoons fresh grated orange peel
 ½ teaspoon ground cinnamon

Pastry
 1 Butter Flavor CRISCO® Stick or 1 cup Butter Flavor CRISCO®
    all-vegetable shortening
 ¼ cup granulated sugar
 3 tablespoons milk
 1 tablespoon rosewater* or water
 2 cups all-purpose flour
    Confectioners' sugar

Rosewater is available at Middle Eastern markets.

1. For filling, combine dates, water, ¼ cup granulated sugar and almond extract in small saucepan. Bring to boil over medium-high heat. Reduce heat to low; simmer 4 to 5 minutes, stirring often, until mixture becomes thick paste. Stir in orange peel and cinnamon. Remove from heat; cool.

2. Heat oven to 300°F. For pastry, combine 1 cup shortening and ¼ cup granulated sugar in large bowl. Beat at medium speed with electric mixer until well blended. Beat in milk and rosewater. Beat in flour, ¼ cup at a time, until well blended. Knead dough in bowl until dough holds together and is easy to shape.

3. Pinch off walnut-size piece of dough; roll into ball. Pinch sides up to form pot shape. Fill with level tablespoonful of date filling. Pinch dough closed; press to seal. Slightly flatten and smooth top. Place on ungreased baking sheets about 1 inch apart.

4. Bake at 300°F for 16 to 20 minutes or until firm and set. *Do not allow pastries to brown.* Cool on baking sheets 3 minutes; transfer to cooling racks. Sprinkle with confectioners' sugar while still warm. Cool completely.

Makes about 2½ dozen pastries

Note: These cookies are traditionally served in Syria during the Easter Holiday.

Ma'moul (Date Pastries)

Czech Bear Paws

4 cups toasted ground hazelnuts
2 cups all-purpose flour
1 tablespoon unsweetened cocoa powder
1 teaspoon ground cinnamon
½ teaspoon ground nutmeg
¼ teaspoon salt
1 cup (2 sticks) plus 3 teaspoons butter, softened, divided
1 cup powdered sugar
1 egg yolk
½ cup chocolate chips, melted
   Slivered almonds, halved

1. Preheat oven to 350°F. Place hazelnuts, flour, cocoa, cinnamon, nutmeg and salt in medium bowl; stir to combine.

2. Beat 1 cup butter, powdered sugar and egg yolk in large bowl with electric mixer at medium speed until light and fluffy. Gradually add flour mixture. Beat at low speed until soft dough forms.

3. Grease 3 madeleine pans with remaining butter, 1 teaspoon per pan; dust with flour. (If only 1 madeleine pan is available, thoroughly wash, dry, regrease and flour after baking each batch. Cover remaining dough with plastic wrap; let stand at room temperature.) Press level tablespoonfuls of dough into each mold.

4. Bake 12 minutes or until lightly browned. Let cookies stand in pan 3 minutes. Carefully loosen cookies from pan with point of small knife. Invert pan over wire rack; tap lightly to release cookies. Let stand 2 minutes. Turn cookies shell-side up; cool completely.

5. Pipe squiggle of melted chocolate on curved end of each cookie; place slivered almond halves in melted chocolate for claws. Let stand at room temperature 1 hour or until set.

6. Store tightly covered at room temperature.   *Makes about 5 dozen cookies*

Note: These cookies do not freeze well.

Czech Bear Paws

Spicy Lemon Crescents

1 cup (2 sticks) butter or margarine, softened
1½ cups powdered sugar, divided
½ teaspoon lemon extract
½ teaspoon grated lemon zest
2 cups cake flour
½ cup finely chopped almonds, walnuts or pecans
1 teaspoon ground cinnamon
½ teaspoon ground cardamom
½ teaspoon ground nutmeg
1¾ cups "M&M's"® Chocolate Mini Baking Bits

Preheat oven to 375°F. Lightly grease cookie sheets; set aside. In large bowl cream butter and ½ cup sugar; add lemon extract and zest until well blended. In medium bowl combine flour, nuts, cinnamon, cardamom and nutmeg; add to creamed mixture until well blended. Stir in "M&M's"® Chocolate Mini Baking Bits. Using 1 tablespoon of dough at a time, form into crescent shapes; place about 2 inches apart onto prepared cookie sheets. Bake 12 to 14 minutes or until edges are golden. Cool 2 minutes on cookie sheets. Gently roll warm crescents in remaining 1 cup sugar. Cool completely on wire racks. Store in tightly covered container.

Makes about 2 dozen cookies

Spicy Lemon Crescents

Cinnamon Chips Gems

1 cup (2 sticks) butter or margarine, softened
2 packages (3 ounces each) cream cheese, softened
2 cups all-purpose flour
½ cup sugar
⅓ cup ground toasted almonds
2 eggs
1 can (14 ounces) sweetened condensed milk
1 teaspoon vanilla extract
1⅓ cups HERSHEY'S Cinnamon Chips, divided

1. Beat butter and cream cheese in large bowl until well blended; stir in flour, sugar and almonds. Cover; refrigerate about 1 hour.

2. Divide dough into 4 equal parts. Shape each part into 12 smooth balls. Place each ball in small muffin cup (1¾ inches in diameter); press evenly on bottom and up sides of each cup.

3. Heat oven to 375°F. Beat eggs in small bowl. Add sweetened condensed milk and vanilla; mix well. Place 7 cinnamon chips in bottom of each cookie shell; fill a generous ¾ full with sweetened condensed milk mixture.

4. Bake 18 to 20 minutes or until tops are puffed and just beginning to turn golden brown. Cool 3 minutes. Sprinkle about 15 chips on top of each cookie. Cool completely in pan on wire rack. Remove from pan using small metal spatula or sharp knife. Store tightly covered at room temperature.

Makes 4 dozen cookies

Cinnamon Chips Gems

Canned Peanut Butter Candy Cookies

¾ **cup chunky peanut butter**
½ **cup (1 stick) butter, softened**
 1 **cup packed light brown sugar**
½ **teaspoon baking powder**
½ **teaspoon baking soda**
 1 **egg**
1½ **teaspoons vanilla**
1¼ **cups all-purpose flour**
 2 **cups quartered miniature peanut butter cups**
⅓ **cup milk chocolate chips or chopped milk chocolate bar**

1. Beat peanut butter and butter in large bowl with electric mixer at medium speed until well blended. Beat in brown sugar, baking powder and baking soda until blended. Beat in egg and vanilla until well blended. Beat in flour at low speed just until mixed. Stir in peanut butter cups. Cover and refrigerate 1 hour or until firm.

2. Preheat oven to 375°F. For test cookie, measure inside diameter of container. Form ⅓ cup dough into ¼-inch-thick disc, about 2 inches in diameter less than the diameter of container. (One-third cup dough patted into 4-inch disc yields 5-inch cookie. Measure amount of dough used and diameter of cookie before and after baking. Make adjustments before making remaining cookies.)

3. Place dough on ungreased cookie sheets. Bake 10 minutes or until lightly browned. Remove to wire racks; cool completely.

4. Place chocolate chips in small resealable plastic food storage bag; seal bag. Microwave at MEDIUM (50% power) 1 minute. Turn bag over; microwave at MEDIUM 1 minute or until melted. Knead bag until chocolate is smooth. Cut off very tiny corner of bag; pipe chocolate decoratively onto cookies. Let stand until chocolate is set.

5. Stack cookies between layers of waxed paper in container. Store loosely covered at room temperature up to 1 week. *Makes 9 (5-inch) cookies*

Canned Peanut Butter Candy Cookies

Snow-on-the-Mountain Cookies

COOKIES
  1¼ **Butter Flavor CRISCO® Sticks or 1¼ cups Butter Flavor CRISCO®
      all-vegetable shortening**
  1 **cup sugar**
  2 **eggs**
  1 **tablespoon vanilla**
  4 **cups all-purpose flour**
  1 **teaspoon salt**
  2 **cups (12-ounce package) semisweet chocolate chips**
  1 **cup chopped walnuts**

GLAZE
  1⅔ **cups (10-ounce package) vanilla milk chips**
  2 to 5 **tablespoons whipping cream or 1 to 3 tablespoons milk**

1. Heat oven to 325°F. Place sheets of foil on countertop for cooling cookies. For cookies, combine 1¼ cups shortening and sugar in large bowl. Beat at medium speed of electric mixer until well blended. Beat in eggs and vanilla.

2. Combine flour and salt. Add gradually to creamed mixture at low speed. Beat until well blended. Stir in chocolate chips and nuts with spoon. Shape dough into 1-inch balls. Shape top of ball into cone or mountain shape. Place 1 inch apart on ungreased baking sheet.

3. Bake at 325°F for 10 to 12 minutes or until light golden brown around bottom edge. *Do not overbake.* Cool on baking sheet 2 minutes. Remove cookies to foil to cool completely.

4. For glaze (prepare while cookies are baking), soften vanilla milk chips (see Melting/Drizzling Procedure). Add enough whipping cream to make medium glaze. Heat and stir until smooth. Spoon or drizzle 1 teaspoonful over top of each warm cookie. Cool completely. *Makes about 6 dozen cookies*

Melting/Drizzling Procedure: For melting or drizzling, choose one of these easy methods. Start with chips and Butter Flavor Crisco® all-vegetable shortening (if called for), then: place in microwave-safe measuring cup or bowl. Microwave at 50% (MEDIUM). Stir after 1 minute. Repeat until smooth. **OR,** place in heavy resealable plastic sandwich bag. Seal. Microwave at 50% (MEDIUM). Check every minute until melted. Knead bag until smooth. Cut tiny tip off corner of bag. Squeeze out to drizzle. **OR,** place in small saucepan. Melt on range top on very low heat. Stir until smooth.

Snow-on-the-Mountain Cookies

cookie cutouts

Lemony Butter Cookies

½ cup (1 stick) butter, softened
½ cup sugar
1 egg
1½ cups all-purpose flour
2 tablespoons fresh lemon juice
1 teaspoon grated lemon peel
½ teaspoon baking powder
⅛ teaspoon salt
  Additional sugar

Beat butter and sugar in large bowl with electric mixer at medium speed until creamy. Beat in egg until light and fluffy. Mix in flour, lemon juice, lemon peel, baking powder and salt. Cover; refrigerate about 2 hours or until firm.

Preheat oven to 350°F. Roll out dough, a small portion at a time, on well-floured surface to ¼-inch thickness. (Keep remaining dough in refrigerator.) Cut dough with 3-inch round or fluted cookie cutter. Transfer cutouts to ungreased cookie sheets. Sprinkle with sugar.

Bake 8 to 10 minutes or until edges are lightly browned. Cool 1 minute on cookie sheets. Remove to wire racks; cool completely. Store in airtight container.

Makes about 2½ dozen cookies

Lemony Butter Cookies

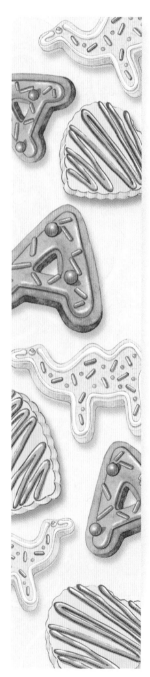

Ultimate Sugar Cookies

1¼ cups granulated sugar
   1 Butter Flavor CRISCO® Stick or 1 cup Butter Flavor CRISCO®
      all-vegetable shortening
   2 eggs
   ¼ cup light corn syrup or regular pancake syrup
   1 tablespoon vanilla
   3 cups plus 4 tablespoons all-purpose flour, divided
   ¾ teaspoon baking powder
   ½ teaspoon baking soda
   ½ teaspoon salt
      Decorations of your choice: granulated sugar, colored sugar
         crystals, decors, frosting, candies, chips, nuts, raisins,
         decorating gel

1. Combine sugar and 1 cup shortening in large bowl. Beat at medium speed of electric mixer until well blended. Add eggs, syrup and vanilla. Beat until well blended and fluffy.

2. Combine 3 cups flour, baking powder, baking soda and salt. Add gradually to creamed mixture at low speed. Mix until well blended. Divide dough into 4 quarters. (Tip: For well-defined cookie edges, or if dough is too sticky or too soft to roll, do the following: Wrap each quarter of dough with plastic wrap. Refrigerate 1 hour. Keep dough balls refrigerated until ready to roll.)

3. Heat oven to 375°F. Place sheets of foil on countertop for cooling cookies. Spread 1 tablespoon flour on large sheet of waxed paper. Place one fourth of dough on paper. Flatten slightly with hands. Turn dough over and cover with another large sheet of waxed paper. Roll dough to ¼-inch thickness. Remove top sheet of waxed paper.

4. Cut out cookies with floured cutter. Transfer to ungreased baking sheet with large pancake turner. Place 2 inches apart. Roll out remaining dough. Sprinkle with granulated sugar, colored sugar crystals, decors or leave plain to frost or decorate when cooled.

5. Bake one baking sheet at a time at 375°F for 5 to 9 minutes, depending on size of cookies. (Bake smaller, thinner cookies closer to 5 minutes, larger cookies closer to 9 minutes.) *Do not overbake.* Cool 2 minutes on baking sheet. Remove cookies to foil to cool completely, then frost if desired.   *Makes about 3 to 4 dozen cookies*

Ultimate Sugar Cookies

Finnish Spice Cookies

2 cups all-purpose flour
1½ teaspoons ground ginger
1½ teaspoons ground cinnamon
½ teaspoon ground cardamom
½ teaspoon ground cloves
⅔ cup packed light brown sugar
½ cup (1 stick) butter, softened
½ teaspoon baking soda
3 to 5 tablespoons hot water
Royal Icing (recipe follows)

1. Place flour, ginger, cinnamon, cardamom and cloves in medium bowl; stir to combine.

2. Beat brown sugar and butter in large bowl until light and fluffy. Dissolve baking soda in 3 tablespoons water. Beat into butter mixture. Gradually add flour mixture. Beat until dough forms. (If dough is too crumbly, add more water, 1 tablespoon at a time, until dough holds together.) Form dough into 2 discs; wrap in plastic wrap and refrigerate until firm, 30 minutes or overnight.

3. Preheat oven to 375°F. Grease cookie sheets; set aside.

4. Working with 1 disc at a time, roll out dough on lightly floured surface to ⅛-inch thickness. Cut dough with floured 3-inch pig-shaped cookie cutter or desired cookie cutter. Place cutouts 1 inch apart on prepared cookie sheets. Gently press dough trimmings together; reroll and cut out more cookies.

5. Bake 8 to 10 minutes or until firm and lightly browned. Remove cookies to wire racks; cool completely.

6. Prepare Royal Icing. Spoon icing into pastry bag fitted with writing tip. Decorate cooled cookies with icing. Let stand at room temperature 1 hour or until set. Store tightly covered at room temperature or freeze up to 3 months.

Makes about 5 dozen cookies

Royal Icing: Beat 1 room-temperature egg white with electric mixer at high speed until foamy. Gradually add 2 cups sifted powdered sugar and ½ teaspoon almond extract; beat at low speed until moistened. Increase mixer speed to high and beat until icing is stiff. (Beat in up to ½ cup additional powdered sugar if necessary to reach proper consistency.)

Finnish Spice Cookies

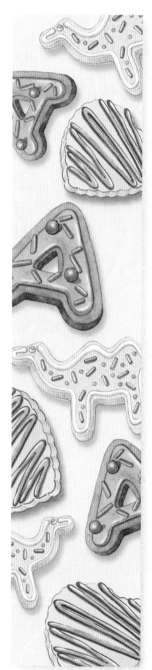

Black & White Hearts

1 cup (2 sticks) butter, softened
¾ cup sugar
1 package (3 ounces) cream cheese, softened
1 egg
1½ teaspoons vanilla
3 cups all-purpose flour
1 cup semisweet chocolate chips
2 tablespoons shortening

1. Combine butter, sugar, cream cheese, egg and vanilla in large bowl. Beat with electric mixer at medium speed, scraping bowl often, until light and fluffy. Add flour; beat until well mixed. Divide dough in half; wrap each half in waxed paper. Refrigerate 2 hours or until firm.

2. Preheat oven to 375°F. Roll out dough to ⅛-inch thickness on lightly floured surface. Cut dough with lightly floured 2-inch heart-shaped cookie cutter. Place cutouts 1 inch apart on ungreased cookie sheets.

3. Bake 7 to 10 minutes or until edges are very lightly browned. Remove immediately to wire racks to cool completely.

4. Melt chocolate chips and shortening in small saucepan over very low heat 4 to 6 minutes or until melted. Dip half of each heart into melted chocolate. Refrigerate on cookie sheets or trays lined with waxed paper until chocolate is firm. Store, covered, in refrigerator. *Makes about 3½ dozen*

Black & White Hearts

Autumn Leaves

1½ cups (3 sticks) unsalted butter, softened
¾ cup packed light brown sugar
½ teaspoon vanilla
3½ cups all-purpose flour
1 teaspoon ground cinnamon
½ teaspoon salt
⅛ teaspoon ground ginger
⅛ teaspoon ground cloves
2 tablespoons unsweetened cocoa powder
Yellow, orange and red food colorings
⅓ cup semisweet chocolate chips

1. Beat butter, brown sugar and vanilla in large bowl with electric mixer at medium speed until light and fluffy. Add flour, cinnamon, salt, ginger and cloves; beat at low speed until well blended.

2. Divide dough into 5 equal sections; reserve 1 section. Stir cocoa into 1 section until well blended. (If dough is too dry and will not hold together, add 1 teaspoon water; beat until well blended and dough forms ball.) Stir yellow food coloring into 1 section until well blended. Repeat with remaining 2 sections and orange and red food colorings.

3. Preheat oven to 350°F. Lightly grease cookie sheets. Working with half of each dough color, press colors together lightly. Roll out dough on lightly floured surface to ¼-inch thickness. Cut dough with leaf-shaped cookie cutters of various shapes and sizes. Place cutouts 2 inches apart on prepared cookie sheets. Repeat with remaining dough sections and scraps.

4. Bake 10 to 15 minutes or until edges are lightly browned. Remove to wire racks; cool completely.

5. Place chocolate chips in small resealable plastic food storage bag; seal. Microwave at HIGH 1 minute; knead bag lightly. Microwave at HIGH for additional 30-second intervals until chips are completely melted, kneading bag after each 30-second interval. Cut off very tiny corner of bag. Pipe chocolate onto cookies in vein patterns. *Makes about 2 dozen cookies*

Autumn Leaves

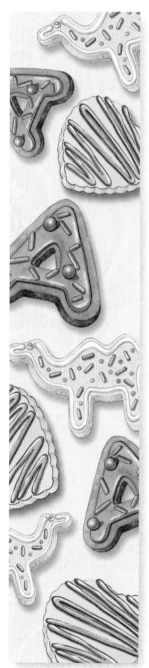

Chocolate-Raspberry Kolacky

> **2 squares (1 ounce each) semisweet chocolate, coarsely chopped**
> **1 ½ cups all-purpose flour**
> **¼ teaspoon baking soda**
> **¼ teaspoon salt**
> **½ cup (1 stick) butter, softened**
> **3 ounces cream cheese or light cream cheese, softened**
> **⅓ cup granulated sugar**
> **1 teaspoon vanilla**
> **Seedless raspberry jam**
> **Powdered sugar**

Place chocolate in small microwavable bowl. Microwave at HIGH 1 to 1 ½ minutes or until chocolate is melted, stirring after 1 minute. Let cool slightly.

Combine flour, baking soda and salt in small bowl; stir well. Beat butter and cream cheese in large bowl with electric mixer at medium speed until well blended. Beat in granulated sugar until light and fluffy. Beat in vanilla and melted chocolate. Gradually add flour mixture. Beat at low speed just until blended. Divide dough in half; flatten each half into disc. Wrap separately in plastic wrap. Refrigerate 1 to 2 hours or until firm.

Preheat oven to 375°F. Lightly grease cookie sheets. Roll out each dough disc on well-floured surface to ¼- to ⅛-inch thickness. Cut dough with 3-inch round cookie cutter. Place cutouts 2 inches apart on prepared cookie sheets. Place rounded ½ teaspoon jam in center of each circle. Bring three edges of dough circles up over jam; pinch edges together to seal, leaving center of triangle slightly open.

Bake 10 minutes or until set. Let cookies stand on cookie sheets 2 minutes. Remove cookies to wire racks; cool completely. Just before serving, sprinkle with powdered sugar. Store tightly covered in refrigerator; let stand 30 minutes at room temperature before serving. *Makes about 1 ½ dozen cookies*

Note: These cookies do not freeze well.

Chocolate-Raspberry Kolacky Cups: Fit dough circles into greased mini-muffin cups; fill with heaping teaspoonful jam. Bake 10 minutes or until set. Let pans stand on wire racks; cool completely. Dust with powdered sugar before serving.

Chocolate-Raspberry Kolacky

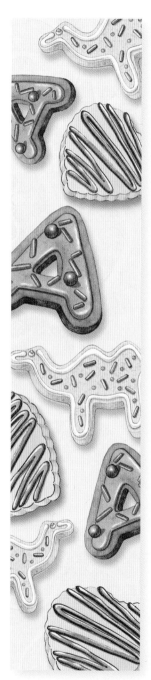

"M&M's"® Jam Sandwiches

½ cup (1 stick) butter, softened
¾ cup granulated sugar
1 large egg
1 teaspoon almond extract
½ teaspoon vanilla extract
1⅓ cups all-purpose flour
¼ teaspoon baking powder
¼ teaspoon salt
   Powdered sugar
½ cup seedless raspberry jam
½ cup "M&M's"® Chocolate Mini Baking Bits

In large bowl cream butter and sugar until light and fluffy; beat in egg, almond extract and vanilla. In small bowl combine flour, baking powder and salt; blend into creamed mixture. Wrap and refrigerate dough 2 to 3 hours. Preheat oven to 375°F. Working with half the dough at a time on lightly floured surface, roll to ⅛-inch thickness. Cut into desired shapes using 3-inch cookie cutters. Cut out equal numbers of each shape. (If dough becomes too soft, refrigerate several minutes before continuing.) Cut 1½- to 2-inch centers out of half the cookies of each shape. Reroll trimmings and cut out more cookies. Using rigid spatula, carefully transfer shapes to ungreased cookie sheets. Bake 7 to 9 minutes. Cool on cookie sheets 1 to 2 minutes; cool completely on wire racks. Sprinkle powdered sugar on cookies with holes. Spread about 1 teaspoon jam on flat side of whole cookies, spreading almost to edges. Place cookies with holes, flat side down, over jam. Place "M&M's"® Chocolate Mini Baking Bits over jam in holes. Store between layers of waxed paper in tightly covered container.

Makes 1 dozen sandwich cookies

"M&M's"® Jam Sandwiches

Moravian Spice Crisps

⅓ cup shortening
⅓ cup packed brown sugar
¼ cup unsulfured molasses
¼ cup dark corn syrup
1¾ to 2 cups all-purpose flour, divided
2 teaspoons ground ginger
1¼ teaspoons baking soda
1 teaspoon ground cinnamon
½ teaspoon ground cloves
Powdered sugar

1. Melt shortening in small saucepan over low heat. Remove from heat; stir in brown sugar, molasses and corn syrup. Set aside to cool.

2. Place 1½ cups flour, ginger, baking soda, cinnamon and cloves in large bowl; stir to combine. Beat in shortening mixture. Gradually beat in remaining ¼ cup flour to form stiff dough.

3. Knead dough on lightly floured surface, adding more flour if dough is too sticky. Form dough into 2 discs; wrap in plastic wrap and refrigerate 30 minutes or until firm.

4. Preheat oven to 350°F. Grease cookie sheets; set aside. Working with 1 disc at a time, roll out dough on lightly floured surface to ¹⁄₁₆-inch thickness.

5. Cut dough with floured 2⅜-inch cookie cutter. (If dough becomes too soft, refrigerate several minutes before continuing.) Gently press dough trimmings together; reroll and cut out more cookies. Place cutouts ½ inch apart on prepared cookie sheets.

6. Bake 8 minutes or until firm and lightly browned. Remove cookies to wire racks; cool completely.

7. Place small strips of cardboard or parchment paper over cookies; dust with sifted powdered sugar. Carefully remove cardboard.   *Makes about 6 dozen cookies*

Moravian Spice Crisps

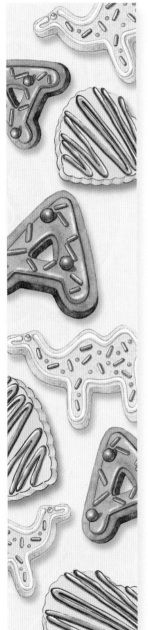

Chocolate and Peanut Butter Hearts

Chocolate Cookie Dough (page 130)
1 cup sugar
½ cup creamy peanut butter
½ cup shortening
1 egg
3 tablespoons milk
1 teaspoon vanilla
2 cups all-purpose flour
1 teaspoon baking powder
¼ teaspoon salt

1. Prepare and chill Chocolate Cookie Dough as directed.

2. Beat sugar, peanut butter and shortening until fluffy. Add egg, milk and vanilla; mix well. Combine flour, baking powder and salt. Beat flour mixture into peanut butter mixture until well blended. Shape dough into disc. Wrap in plastic wrap; refrigerate 1 to 2 hours or until firm.

3. Preheat oven to 350°F. Grease cookie sheets. Roll peanut butter dough on floured waxed paper to ⅛-inch thickness. Cut dough using 3-inch heart-shaped cookie cutter. Place cutouts on prepared cookie sheets. Repeat with chocolate dough.

4. Use smaller heart-shaped cookie cutter to remove small section from centers of hearts. Place small peanut butter hearts into large chocolate hearts; place small chocolate hearts into large peanut butter hearts. Press together lightly.

5. Bake 12 to 14 minutes or until edges are lightly browned. Remove to wire racks; cool completely.   *Makes 4 dozen cookies*

Chocolate and Peanut Butter Hearts

Chocolate Cookie Dough

1 cup (2 sticks) butter, softened
1 cup sugar
1 egg
1 teaspoon vanilla
2 ounces semisweet chocolate, melted
2¼ cups all-purpose flour
1 teaspoon baking powder
¼ teaspoon salt

1. Beat butter and sugar in large bowl with electric mixer at high speed until fluffy. Beat in egg and vanilla. Add melted chocolate; mix well.

2. Add flour, baking powder and salt; mix well. Cover; refrigerate about 2 hours or until firm.

Old-Fashioned Molasses Cookies

4 cups sifted all-purpose flour
2 teaspoons ARM & HAMMER® Baking Soda
2 teaspoons ground ginger
1 teaspoon ground cinnamon
⅛ teaspoon salt
1½ cups molasses
½ cup butter-flavored shortening
⅓ cup boiling water
Sugar

In medium bowl, combine flour, Baking Soda, spices and salt. In large bowl, mix molasses, shortening and water. Add dry ingredients to molasses mixture; blend well. Cover; refrigerate until firm, about 2 hours. Roll out dough ¼ inch thick on well-floured surface. Cut out with 3½-inch cookie cutters; sprinkle with sugar. Place 2 inches apart on ungreased cookie sheets. Bake in preheated 375°F oven about 12 minutes. Remove to wire racks to cool.   *Makes about 3 dozen cookies*

Rugelach

1 package (8 ounces) PHILADELPHIA® Cream Cheese, softened
1¼ cups (2½ sticks) butter or margarine, divided
2¼ cups flour
1 cup finely chopped PLANTERS® Walnuts
½ cup sugar
1 tablespoon ground cinnamon, divided
Raspberry preserves
2 tablespoons sugar

BEAT cream cheese and 1 cup of the butter with electric mixer on medium speed until well blended. Gradually add flour, mixing until blended. (Dough will be very soft and sticky.) Divide dough into 4 portions; place each on sheet of plastic wrap. Shape each portion into 1-inch-thick circle, using floured hands. Wrap plastic wrap around each circle to enclose. Refrigerate overnight.

LINE greased cookie sheet with foil or parchment paper. Roll each portion of dough into 11-inch circle on lightly floured surface, lifting dough occasionally to add more flour to work surface to prevent sticking. Melt remaining ¼ cup butter. Mix walnuts, ½ cup sugar and 2 teaspoons of the cinnamon. Brush surface of dough with butter; sprinkle evenly with walnut mixture.

CUT each circle into 8 wedges. Spoon ½ teaspoon preserves at wide end of each wedge; roll up from wide end of wedge. Place on cookie sheet; shape into crescents. Brush tops with additional melted butter; sprinkle with combined remaining 1 teaspoon cinnamon and 2 tablespoons sugar.

BAKE at 350°F for 20 to 23 minutes or until light golden brown. Immediately remove from cookie sheet. Cool on wire rack. *Makes 32 cookies*

Note: For smaller cookies, cut each circle of dough into 16 wedges. Continue as directed. Makes 64 cookies.

Prep Time: 1 hour
Total Time: 9 hours 23 minutes

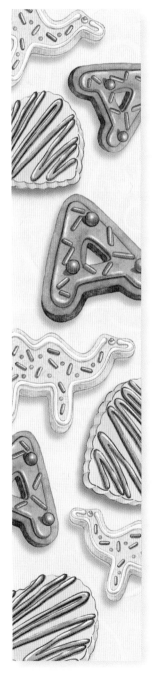

Butterfly Cookies

2¼ cups all-purpose flour
¼ teaspoon salt
1 cup sugar
¾ cup (1½ sticks) butter, softened
1 egg
1 teaspoon vanilla
1 teaspoon almond extract
White frosting, assorted food colorings, colored sugars, assorted
small decors, gummy fruit and hard candies for decoration

1. Combine flour and salt in medium bowl; set aside.

2. Beat sugar and butter in large bowl with electric mixer at medium speed until fluffy. Beat in egg, vanilla and almond extract. Gradually add flour mixture. Beat at low speed until well blended. Divide dough in half. Cover; refrigerate 30 minutes or until firm.

3. Preheat oven to 350°F. Grease cookie sheets. Roll half of dough on lightly floured surface to ¼-inch thickness. Cut dough with butterfly cookie cutters. Repeat with remaining dough. Transfer cutouts to ungreased cookie sheets.

4. Bake 12 to 15 minutes or until edges are lightly browned. Remove to wire racks; cool completely.

5. Tint portions of white frosting with assorted food colorings. Spread desired colors of frosting over cookies. Decorate as desired.   *Makes about 20 to 22 cookies*

Butterfly Cookies

Peanut Butter Cut-Out Cookies

½ cup (1 stick) butter or margarine
1 cup REESE'S® Peanut Butter Chips
⅔ cup packed light brown sugar
1 egg
¾ teaspoon vanilla extract
1⅓ cups all-purpose flour
¾ teaspoon baking soda
½ cup finely chopped pecans
   Chocolate Chip Glaze (recipe follows)

1. Place butter and peanut butter chips in medium saucepan; cook over low heat, stirring constantly, until melted. Pour into large bowl; add brown sugar, egg and vanilla, beating until well blended. Stir in flour, baking soda and pecans, blending well. Refrigerate 15 to 20 minutes or until firm enough to roll.

2. Heat oven to 350°F.

3. Roll a small portion of dough at a time on lightly floured board, or between 2 pieces of wax paper, to ¼-inch thickness. (Keep remaining dough in refrigerator.) With cookie cutters, cut dough into desired shapes; place on ungreased cookie sheets.

4. Bake 7 to 8 minutes or until almost set (do not overbake). Cool 1 minute; remove from cookie sheets to wire racks. Cool completely. Drizzle Chocolate Chip Glaze onto each cookie; allow to set.   *Makes about 3 dozen cookies*

Chocolate Chip Glaze: Place 1 cup HERSHEY'S Semi-Sweet Chocolate Chips and 1 tablespoon shortening (do not use butter, margarine spread or oil) in small microwave-safe bowl. Microwave at HIGH (100%) 1 minute; stir. If necessary, microwave at HIGH an additional 15 seconds at a time, stirring after each heating, just until chips are melted and mixture is smooth.

Peanut Butter Cut-Out Cookies

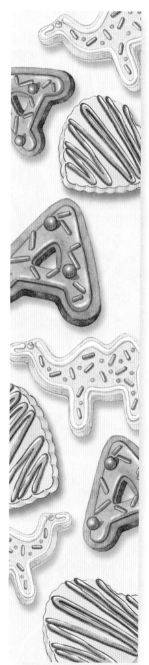

Jam-Up Oatmeal Cookies

**1 Butter Flavor CRISCO® Stick or 1 cup Butter Flavor CRISCO®
  all-vegetable shortening plus additional for greasing**
1½ cups firmly packed brown sugar
  2 eggs
  2 teaspoons almond extract
  2 cups all-purpose flour
  1 teaspoon baking powder
  1 teaspoon salt
  ½ teaspoon baking soda
2½ cups quick oats (not instant or old-fashioned), uncooked
  1 cup finely chopped pecans
  1 jar (12 ounces) strawberry jam
  Sugar for sprinkling

1. Combine 1 cup shortening and brown sugar in large bowl. Beat at medium speed of electric mixer until well blended. Beat in eggs and almond extract.

2. Combine flour, baking powder, salt and baking soda. Add to shortening mixture at low speed until just blended. Stir in oats and chopped nuts with spoon. Cover and refrigerate at least 1 hour.

3. Heat oven to 350°F. Grease baking sheets with shortening. Place sheets of foil on countertop for cooling cookies.

4. Roll out dough, half at a time, to about ¼-inch thickness on floured surface. Cut out with 2½-inch round cookie cutter. Place 1 teaspoonful of jam in center of half of the rounds. Top with remaining rounds. Press edges to seal. Prick centers; sprinkle with sugar. Place 1 inch apart on baking sheets.

5. Bake one baking sheet at a time at 350°F for 12 to 15 minutes or until lightly browned. *Do not overbake.* Cool 2 minutes on baking sheets. Remove cookies to foil to cool completely.   *Makes about 2 dozen cookies*

Jam-Up Oatmeal Cookies

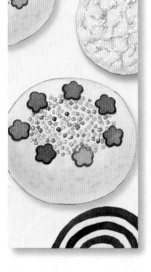

refrigerator cookies

Pinwheel Cookies

½ cup shortening plus additional for greasing
⅓ cup plus 1 tablespoon butter, softened and divided
2 egg yolks
½ teaspoon vanilla extract
1 package DUNCAN HINES® Moist Deluxe® Fudge Marble Cake Mix

1. Combine ½ cup shortening, ⅓ cup butter, egg yolks and vanilla extract in large bowl. Mix at low speed of electric mixer until blended. Set aside cocoa packet from cake mix. Gradually add cake mix. Blend well.

2. Divide dough in half. Add cocoa packet and remaining 1 tablespoon butter to one half of dough. Knead until well blended and chocolate colored.

3. Roll out yellow dough between two pieces of waxed paper into 18×12×⅛-inch rectangle. Repeat for chocolate dough. Remove top pieces of waxed paper from chocolate and yellow doughs. Place yellow dough directly on top of chocolate dough. Remove remaining layers of waxed paper. Roll up jelly-roll fashion, beginning at wide side. Refrigerate 2 hours.

4. Preheat oven to 350°F. Grease baking sheets.

5. Cut dough into ⅛-inch slices. Place sliced dough 1 inch apart on prepared baking sheets. Bake at 350°F for 9 to 11 minutes or until lightly browned. Cool 5 minutes on baking sheets. Remove to cooling racks.

Makes about 3½ dozen cookies

Pinwheel Cookies

Orange Dreams

2½ cups all-purpose flour
¼ teaspoon baking powder
¼ teaspoon baking soda
¼ teaspoon salt
1 cup (2 sticks) unsalted butter, softened
2½ cups powdered sugar, divided
1 egg
4 tablespoons orange juice, divided
1½ tablespoons plus 1 teaspoon finely grated orange peel, divided
2 teaspoons vanilla
1 teaspoon lemon juice
1 teaspoon orange extract
Red and yellow food coloring (optional)
1 container (16 ounces) vanilla frosting

1. Combine flour, baking powder, baking soda and salt in small bowl. Beat butter and 1 cup powdered sugar in large bowl with electric mixer at medium speed 1 minute or until creamy. Add egg, 2 tablespoons orange juice, 1½ tablespoons orange peel, vanilla, lemon juice and orange extract; beat until well blended. Gradually stir in flour mixture; mix well.

2. Shape dough into 2 logs about 2 inches in diameter on lightly floured work surface. Wrap each log tightly in waxed paper. Refrigerate logs 3 hours or overnight.

3. Preheat oven to 350°F. Grease cookie sheets. Cut logs into ¼-inch-thick slices; place 1 inch apart on prepared sheets. Bake 10 minutes or until lightly brown around edges. Let cookies cool on cookie sheets 2 minutes. Transfer to wire racks; cool completely.

4. Combine remaining 1½ cups powdered sugar, 2 tablespoons orange juice and 1 teaspoon orange peel in medium bowl; beat until blended. Add additional orange juice, if necessary, for desired consistency. Add a few drops red and yellow food coloring, if desired; mix until desired orange color. Glaze tops of cookies; let stand 1 hour or until glaze is set. Frost half of cookie bottoms with vanilla frosting; place second cookie on frosting to make sandwich cookie. Store loosely covered in single layer for up to 1 week or in freezer for 1 month.

Makes about 2 dozen sandwich cookies

Orange Dreams

Cinnamon Roll Cookies

Cinnamon Mixture
   4 tablespoons granulated sugar
   1 tablespoon ground cinnamon

Cookie Dough
   **1 Butter Flavor CRISCO® Stick or 1 cup Butter Flavor CRISCO®
      all-vegetable shortening**
   1 cup firmly packed light brown sugar
   2 large eggs
   1 teaspoon vanilla
   3 cups all-purpose flour
   2 teaspoons baking powder
   ½ teaspoon salt
   1 teaspoon ground cinnamon

1. For cinnamon mixture, combine granulated sugar and 1 tablespoon cinnamon in small bowl; mix well. Set aside.

2. For cookie dough, combine 1 cup shortening and brown sugar in large bowl. Beat at medium speed with electric mixer until well blended. Beat in eggs and vanilla until well blended.

3. Combine flour, baking powder, salt and 1 teaspoon cinnamon in small bowl. Add to creamed mixture; mix well.

4. Turn dough onto sheet of waxed paper. Spread dough into 9×6-inch rectangle using rubber spatula. Sprinkle with 4 tablespoons cinnamon mixture to within 1 inch of edges. Roll up jelly-roll style into log. Dust log with remaining cinnamon mixture. Wrap tightly in plastic wrap; refrigerate 4 hours or overnight.

5. Heat oven to 375°F. Spray cookie sheets with CRISCO® No-Stick Cooking Spray.

6. Slice dough ¼ inch thick. Place on prepared cookie sheets. Bake at 350°F for 8 minutes or until lightly browned on top. Cool on cookie sheets 4 minutes; transfer to cooling racks. *Makes about 5 dozen cookies*

Kitchen Hint: Be careful when working with this dough. It is a stiff dough and can crack easily when rolling. Roll the dough slowly and smooth any cracks with your finger as you go.

Cinnamon Roll Cookies

Spiced Wafers

½ cup (1 stick) butter, softened
1 cup sugar
1 egg
2 tablespoons milk
1 teaspoon vanilla
1¾ cups all-purpose flour
2 teaspoons baking powder
1 teaspoon ground cinnamon
½ teaspoon ground nutmeg
¼ teaspoon ground cloves
Red hot candies or red colored sugar for garnish (optional)

Beat butter in large bowl with electric mixer at medium speed until smooth. Add sugar; beat until well blended. Add egg, milk and vanilla; beat until well blended.

Combine flour, baking powder, cinnamon, nutmeg and cloves in large bowl. Gradually add flour mixture to butter mixture at low speed, blending well after each addition.

Shape dough into 2 logs, each about 2 inches in diameter and 6 inches long. Wrap each log in plastic wrap. Refrigerate 2 to 3 hours or overnight.

Preheat oven to 350°F. Grease cookie sheets. Cut logs into ¼-inch-thick slices; decorate with candies or colored sugar, if desired. (Or, leave plain and decorate with icing after baking.) Place at least 2 inches apart on cookie sheets.

Bake 11 to 13 minutes or until edges are light brown. Transfer to wire racks to cool. Store in airtight container. *Makes about 4 dozen cookies*

Spiced Wafers

Choco-Coco Pecan Crisps

>   1 cup packed light brown sugar
> ½ cup (1 stick) butter, softened
>   1 egg
>   1 teaspoon vanilla
> 1 ½ cups all-purpose flour
>   1 cup chopped pecans
> ⅓ cup unsweetened cocoa powder
> ½ teaspoon baking soda
>   1 cup flaked coconut

Beat brown sugar and butter until light and fluffy. Beat in egg and vanilla. Combine flour, pecans, cocoa and baking soda; stir into creamed mixture to form stiff dough. Sprinkle coconut on work surface. Divide dough into 4 parts; shape each part into roll about 1½ inches in diameter. Roll in coconut until thickly coated. Wrap in plastic wrap; refrigerate until firm, at least 1 hour or up to 2 days. Preheat oven to 350°F. Cut rolls into ⅛-inch slices; place on ungreased cookie sheets. Bake 10 to 13 minutes or until firm. Remove to wire racks to cool.   *Makes about 6 dozen cookies*

Almond Cream Cheese Cookies

>   1 (3-ounce) package cream cheese, softened
>   1 cup butter, softened
>   1 cup sugar
>   1 egg yolk
>   1 tablespoon milk
> ⅛ teaspoon almond extract
> 2½ cups sifted cake flour
>   1 cup BLUE DIAMOND® Sliced Natural Almonds, toasted

Beat cream cheese with butter and sugar until fluffy. Blend in egg yolk, milk and almond extract. Gradually mix in flour. Gently stir in almonds. (Dough will be sticky.) Divide dough in half; place each half on large sheet of waxed paper. Working through waxed paper, shape each half into 12×1½-inch roll. Chill until very firm.

Preheat oven to 325°F. Cut rolls into ¼-inch slices. Bake on ungreased cookie sheets 10 to 15 minutes or until edges are golden. (Cookies will not brown.) Cool on wire racks.   *Makes about 4 dozen cookies*

Choco-Coco Pecan Crisps

Mini Chip Slice and Bake Cookies

⅓ cup butter or margarine, softened
¾ cup granulated sugar
½ cup packed light brown sugar
1 egg
1 teaspoon vanilla extract
2½ cups all-purpose flour
1 teaspoon baking soda
½ teaspoon baking powder
½ teaspoon salt
2 to 3 tablespoons milk
1 cup HERSHEY'S MINI CHIPS™ Semi-Sweet Chocolate Chips

1. Beat butter, granulated sugar and brown sugar in large bowl on medium speed of mixer until creamy. Add egg and vanilla; beat well. Stir together flour, baking soda, baking powder and salt; gradually add to butter mixture, beating until well blended. Add milk, 1 tablespoon at a time, until dough holds together. Stir in small chocolate chips.

2. Divide dough in half. Shape each half into 1½-inch-thick roll. Wrap tightly in wax paper; refrigerate 5 to 24 hours.

3. Heat oven to 350°F. Lightly grease cookie sheet.

4. Using sharp knife and sawing motion, cut rolls into ¼-inch slices. Place on prepared cookie sheet.

5. Bake 8 to 10 minutes or until set. Remove from cookie sheet to wire rack. Cool completely. *Makes about 6 dozen cookies*

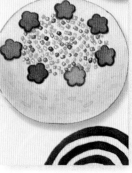

Domino® Sugar Cookies

1 cup DOMINO® Granulated Sugar
1 cup (2 sticks) butter or margarine, softened
1 egg
1 tablespoon vanilla
2¼ cups all-purpose flour
1 teaspoon baking soda
Additional DOMINO® Granulated Sugar

In large bowl, blend sugar and butter. Beat in egg and vanilla until light and fluffy. Mix in flour and baking soda. Divide dough in half. Shape each half into roll about 1½ inches in diameter. Wrap and refrigerate for 1 hour until chilled.* Cut rolls into ¼-inch slices. Place on ungreased baking sheet and sprinkle generously with additional sugar. Bake in 375°F oven for 10 to 12 minutes or until lightly browned around edges. Cool on wire rack.   *Makes about 3 dozen cookies*

**Tip: To chill dough quickly, place in freezer for 30 minutes.*

Peppersass Cookies

2¼ cups flour
½ teaspoon baking soda
½ teaspoon salt
1½ cups sugar, divided
⅔ cup butter or margarine, at room temperature
1 egg
2 teaspoons TABASCO® brand Pepper Sauce
1 teaspoon vanilla extract

Combine flour, baking soda and salt in small bowl. Beat 1 cup sugar and butter in large bowl with electric mixer at low speed until well blended. Add egg, TABASCO® Sauce, vanilla and flour mixture; beat until smooth.

Divide dough in half; place halves on plastic wrap. Shape each half into log about 1½ inches in diameter. Cover and refrigerate until firm, 2 to 3 hours or overnight.

Preheat oven to 350°F. Place remaining ½ cup sugar in shallow dish. Cut dough logs into ¼-inch-thick slices; dip each slice in sugar. Place slices 1 inch apart on ungreased cookie sheets. Bake 10 to 12 minutes or until cookies are golden around edges. Cool on wire racks.   *Makes about 5 dozen cookies*

St. Pat's Pinwheels

1¼ cups granulated sugar
1 cup Butter Flavor CRISCO® all-vegetable shortening or
    1 Butter Flavor CRISCO® Stick
2 eggs
¼ cup light corn syrup or regular pancake syrup
1 tablespoon vanilla
3 cups all-purpose flour plus 2 tablespoons, divided
¾ teaspoon baking powder
½ teaspoon baking soda
½ teaspoon salt
½ teaspoon peppermint extract
Green food color

1. Place sugar and 1 cup shortening in large bowl. Beat at medium speed of electric mixer until blended. Add eggs, syrup and vanilla; beat until well blended and fluffy.

2. Combine 3 cups flour, baking powder, baking soda and salt. Add gradually to shortening mixture, beating at low speed until well blended.

3. Place half of dough in medium bowl. Stir in peppermint extract and food color, a few drops at a time, until desired shade of green. Shape each dough into disk. Wrap with plastic wrap. Refrigerate several hours or until firm.

4. Sprinkle about 1 tablespoon flour on large sheet of waxed paper. Place peppermint dough on floured paper; flatten slightly with hands. Turn dough over; cover with another large sheet of waxed paper. Roll dough into 14×9-inch rectangle. Set aside. Repeat with plain dough.

5. Remove top sheet of waxed paper from both doughs. Invert plain dough onto peppermint dough, aligning edges carefully. Roll layers together lightly. Remove waxed paper from plain dough. Trim dough to form rectangle. Roll up tightly jelly-roll fashion, starting with long side; use bottom sheet of waxed paper as guide and remove paper during rolling. Wrap roll in waxed paper; freeze at least 30 minutes or until very firm.

6. Heat oven to 375°F. Place sheets of foil on countertop for cooling cookies. Remove roll from freezer; remove wrapping. Cut roll into ⅜-inch-thick slices. Place slices 2 inches apart on ungreased baking sheet.

7. Bake one baking sheet at a time at 375°F for 7 to 9 minutes or until edges of cookies are very lightly browned. *Do not overbake.* Cool 2 minutes on baking sheet. Remove cookies to foil to cool completely.   *Makes about 3 dozen cookies*

St. Pat's Pinwheels

Cappuccino Cookies

1 cup (2 sticks) butter, softened
2 cups packed brown sugar
2 tablespoons milk
2 tablespoons instant coffee granules
2 eggs
1 teaspoon rum extract
½ teaspoon vanilla
4 cups all-purpose flour
1 teaspoon baking powder
½ teaspoon ground nutmeg
¼ teaspoon salt
   Chocolate sprinkles or melted semisweet and/or white chocolate chips (optional)

Beat butter in large bowl with electric mixer at medium speed until smooth. Add brown sugar; beat until well blended.

Heat milk in small saucepan over low heat; add coffee granules, stirring to dissolve. Add milk mixture, eggs, rum extract and vanilla to butter mixture. Beat at medium speed until well blended.

Combine flour, baking powder, nutmeg and salt in large bowl. Gradually add flour mixture to butter mixture, beating at low speed after each addition until blended.

Shape dough into 2 logs, about 2 inches in diameter and 8 inches long. (Dough will be soft; sprinkle lightly with flour if too sticky to handle.)

Roll logs in chocolate sprinkles, if desired, coating evenly (⅓ cup sprinkles per roll). Or, leave rolls plain and dip cookies in melted chocolate after baking. Wrap each log in plastic wrap; refrigerate overnight.

Preheat oven to 350°F. Grease cookie sheets. Cut rolls into ¼-inch-thick slices; place 1 inch apart on cookie sheets. (Keep unbaked rolls and sliced cookies chilled until ready to bake.)

Bake 10 to 12 minutes or until edges are lightly browned. Transfer to wire racks to cool. Dip plain cookies in melted semisweet or white chocolate, if desired. Store in airtight container.   *Makes about 5 dozen cookies*

Cappuccino Cookies

Date Pinwheel Cookies

1¼ cups dates, pitted and finely chopped
¾ cup orange juice
½ cup granulated sugar
1 tablespoon butter
3 cups plus 1 tablespoon all-purpose flour, divided
2 teaspoons vanilla, divided
1 cup packed brown sugar
4 ounces cream cheese
¼ cup shortening
2 eggs
1 teaspoon baking soda
½ teaspoon salt

1. Heat dates, orange juice, granulated sugar, butter and 1 tablespoon flour in medium saucepan over medium heat. Cook 10 minutes or until thick, stirring frequently; remove from heat. Stir in 1 teaspoon vanilla; set aside to cool.

2. Beat brown sugar, cream cheese and shortening in large bowl with electric mixer about 3 minutes until light and fluffy. Add eggs and remaining 1 teaspoon vanilla; beat 2 minutes longer.

3. Combine remaining 3 cups flour, baking soda and salt in medium bowl. Add to shortening mixture; stir just until blended. Divide dough in half. Roll one half of dough on lightly floured surface into 12×9-inch rectangle. Spread half of date mixture over dough. Spread evenly, leaving ¼-inch border at top short edge. Starting at short side, tightly roll up dough jelly-roll style. Wrap in plastic wrap; freeze at least 1 hour. Repeat with remaining dough and date mixture.

4. Preheat oven to 350°F. Grease cookie sheets. Unwrap dough. Using heavy thread or dental floss, cut dough into ¼-inch slices. Place slices 1 inch apart on prepared cookie sheets.

5. Bake 12 minutes or until lightly browned. Let cookies stand on cookie sheets 2 minutes. Remove cookies to wire racks; cool completely.

Makes 6 dozen cookies

Date Pinwheel Cookies

Chocolate-Dipped Cinnamon Thins

1 ¼ cups all-purpose flour
1 ½ teaspoons ground cinnamon
¼ teaspoon salt
1 cup (2 sticks) unsalted butter, softened
1 cup powdered sugar
1 egg
1 teaspoon vanilla
4 ounces broken bittersweet chocolate candy bar, melted

1. Combine flour, cinnamon and salt in small bowl; set aside. Beat butter in large bowl with electric mixer at medium speed until light and fluffy. Add powdered sugar; beat well. Add egg and vanilla. Gradually add flour mixture. Beat at low speed just until blended.

2. Place dough on sheet of waxed paper. Using waxed paper to hold dough, roll back and forth to form log, about 12 inches long and 2½ inches in diameter. Securely wrap log in plastic wrap. Refrigerate at least 2 hours or until firm. (Log may be frozen up to 3 months; thaw in refrigerator before baking.)

3. Preheat oven to 350°F. Cut dough into ¼-inch-thick slices. Place 2 inches apart on ungreased cookie sheets. Bake 10 minutes or until set. Let cookies stand on cookie sheets 2 minutes. Remove cookies to wire racks; cool completely.

4. Dip each cookie into chocolate, coating 1 inch up sides. Transfer to wire racks or waxed paper; let stand at cool room temperature about 40 minutes or until chocolate is set.

5. Store cookies between sheets of waxed paper at cool room temperature or in refrigerator.

Makes about 2 dozen cookies

Note: These cookies do not freeze well.

Chocolate-Dipped Cinnamon Thins

Lip-Smacking Lemon Cookies

½ cup (1 stick) butter, softened
1 cup sugar
1 egg
2 tablespoons lemon juice
2 teaspoons grated lemon peel
2 cups all-purpose flour
1 teaspoon baking powder
⅛ teaspoon salt
Dash ground nutmeg

Beat butter in large bowl with electric mixer at medium speed until smooth. Add sugar; beat until well blended. Add egg, lemon juice and peel; beat until well blended.

Combine flour, baking powder, salt and nutmeg in large bowl. Gradually add flour mixture to butter mixture at low speed, blending well after each addition.

Shape dough into 2 logs, each about 1½ inches in diameter and 6½ inches long. Wrap each log in plastic wrap. Refrigerate 2 to 3 hours or up to 3 days.

Preheat oven to 350°F. Grease cookie sheets. Cut logs into ¼-inch-thick slices; place 1 inch apart on cookie sheets.

Bake about 15 minutes or until edges are light brown. Transfer to wire racks to cool. Store in airtight container. *Makes about 4 dozen cookies*

Lip-Smacking Lemon Cookies

Cinnamon Nut Chocolate Spirals

1½ cups all-purpose flour
¼ teaspoon salt
¾ cup sugar, divided
⅓ cup butter, softened
1 egg
1 cup mini semisweet chocolate chips
1 cup very finely chopped walnuts
2 teaspoons ground cinnamon
3 tablespoons butter

Combine flour and salt in small bowl; set aside. Beat ½ cup sugar and ⅓ cup softened butter in large bowl with electric mixer at medium speed until light and fluffy. Beat in egg. Gradually add flour mixture. Dough will be stiff. (If necessary, knead dough by hand until it holds together.)

Roll out dough between 2 sheets of waxed paper into 12×10-inch rectangle. Remove waxed paper from top of rectangle.

Combine chips, walnuts, remaining ¼ cup sugar and cinnamon in medium bowl. Melt 3 tablespoons butter; pour hot melted butter over chocolate chip mixture; mix well. (Chips will partially melt.) Spoon mixture over dough. Spread evenly, leaving ½-inch border on long edges.

Using bottom sheet of waxed paper as guide and starting at long side, tightly roll up dough jelly-roll style, removing waxed paper as you roll. Wrap in plastic wrap; refrigerate 30 minutes to 1 hour.*

Preheat oven to 350°F. Lightly grease cookie sheets. Unwrap dough. Using heavy thread or dental floss, cut dough into ½-inch slices. Place slices 2 inches apart on prepared cookie sheets.

Bake 14 minutes or until edges are light golden brown. Cool completely on wire racks.   *Makes about 2 dozen cookies*

*If dough is chilled longer than 1 hour, slice with sharp, thin knife.

Cinnamon Nut Chocolate Spirals

Chocolate-Peanut Butter Checkerboards

½ cup (1 stick) butter or margarine, softened
1 cup sugar
1 egg
1 teaspoon vanilla extract
1 cup plus 3 tablespoons all-purpose flour, divided
½ teaspoon baking soda
¼ cup HERSHEY'S Cocoa
½ cup REESE'S® Peanut Butter Chips, melted

1. Beat butter, sugar, egg and vanilla in large bowl until fluffy. Add 1 cup flour and baking soda; beat until blended. Remove ¾ cup batter to small bowl; set aside. Add cocoa and remaining 3 tablespoons flour to remaining batter in large bowl; blend well.

2. Place peanut butter chips in small microwave-safe bowl. Microwave at HIGH (100%) 30 seconds or until melted and smooth when stirred. Immediately add to batter in small bowl, stirring until smooth. Divide chocolate dough into four equal parts. Roll each part between plastic wrap or wax paper into log 7 inches long and about 1 inch in diameter. Repeat with peanut butter dough. Wrap each roll individually in waxed paper or plastic wrap. Refrigerate several hours until very firm.

3. Heat oven to 350°F. Remove rolls from waxed paper. Place 1 chocolate roll and 1 peanut butter roll side by side on cutting board. Top each roll with another roll of opposite flavor to make checkerboard pattern. Lightly press rolls together; repeat with remaining four rolls. Working with one checkerboard at a time (keep remaining checkerboard covered and refrigerated), cut into ¼-inch slices. Place on ungreased cookie sheet.

4. Bake 8 to 9 minutes or until peanut butter portion is lightly browned. Cool 1 minute; remove from cookie sheet to wire rack. Cool completely.

Makes about 4½ dozen cookies

Chocolate-Peanut Butter Checkerboards

bar cookies

Chocolatey Raspberry Crumb Bars

   1 cup (2 sticks) butter or margarine, softened
   2 cups all-purpose flour
   ½ cup packed light brown sugar
   ¼ teaspoon salt
   2 cups (12-ounce package) NESTLÉ® TOLL HOUSE® Semi-Sweet
      Chocolate Morsels, *divided*
   1 can (14 ounces) NESTLÉ® CARNATION® Sweetened Condensed Milk
   ½ cup chopped nuts (optional)
   ⅓ cup seedless raspberry jam

PREHEAT oven to 350°F. Grease 13×9-inch baking pan.

BEAT butter in large mixer bowl until creamy. Beat in flour, sugar and salt until crumbly. With floured fingers, press *1¾ cups* crumb mixture onto bottom of prepared baking pan; reserve *remaining* mixture.

BAKE for 10 to 12 minutes or until edges are golden brown.

MICROWAVE *1 cup* morsels and sweetened condensed milk in medium, uncovered, microwave-safe bowl on HIGH (100%) power for 1 minute. STIR. Morsels may retain some of their original shape. If necessary, microwave at additional 10- to 15-second intervals, stirring just until morsels are melted. Spread over hot crust.

STIR nuts into *reserved* flour mixture; sprinkle over chocolate layer. Drop teaspoonfuls of raspberry jam over crumb mixture. Sprinkle with *remaining* morsels.

BAKE for 25 to 30 minutes or until center is set. Cool in pan on wire rack. Cut into bars.   *Makes 3 dozen bars*

Chocolatey Raspberry Crumb Bars

Yellow's Nuts for Nutty Squares

1 cup (2 sticks) plus 2 tablespoons butter, softened and divided
½ cup powdered sugar
2¼ cups all-purpose flour
¼ teaspoon salt
¾ cup granulated sugar
½ cup light corn syrup
2 large eggs, beaten
½ teaspoon vanilla extract
2 cups coarsely chopped mixed nuts
1 cup "M&M's"® Semi-Sweet Chocolate Mini Baking Bits

Preheat oven to 325°F. Lightly grease 13×9-inch baking pan; set aside. In large bowl beat 1 cup (2 sticks) butter and powdered sugar; gradually add flour and salt until well blended. Press dough evenly onto bottom and ½ inch up sides of prepared pan. Bake 25 to 30 minutes or until very light golden brown. In small saucepan melt remaining 2 tablespoons butter; let cool slightly. In large bowl combine melted butter, granulated sugar, corn syrup, eggs and vanilla. Pour filling over partially baked crust; sprinkle with nuts and "M&M's"® Semi-Sweet Chocolate Mini Baking Bits. Return to oven; bake 30 to 35 minutes or until filling is set. Remove pan to wire rack; cool completely. Cut into bars. Store in tightly covered container. *Makes 2 dozen bars*

Buttery Black Raspberry Bars

1 cup butter or margarine
1 cup sugar
2 egg yolks
2 cups all-purpose flour
1 cup chopped walnuts
½ cup SMUCKER'S® Seedless Black Raspberry Jam

Beat butter until soft and creamy. Gradually add sugar, beating until mixture is light and fluffy. Add egg yolks; blend well. Gradually add flour; mix thoroughly. Fold in walnuts.

Spoon half of batter into greased 8-inch square pan; spread evenly. Top with jam; cover with remaining batter.

Bake at 325°F for 1 hour or until lightly browned. Cool and cut into 2×1-inch bars. *Makes 32 bars*

Yellow's Nuts for Nutty Squares

Peanut Butter Chip Triangles

1½ cups all-purpose flour
½ cup packed light brown sugar
½ cup (1 stick) cold butter or margarine
1⅔ cups (10-ounce package) REESE'S® Peanut Butter Chips, divided
1 can (14 ounces) sweetened condensed milk (not evaporated milk)
1 egg, slightly beaten
1 teaspoon vanilla extract
¾ cup chopped walnuts
Powdered sugar (optional)

1. Heat oven to 350°F. Stir together flour and brown sugar in medium bowl. Cut in butter with pastry blender or fork until mixture resembles coarse crumbs. Stir in ½ cup peanut butter chips. Press mixture into bottom of ungreased 13×9×2-inch baking pan. Bake 15 minutes.

2. Meanwhile, combine sweetened condensed milk, egg and vanilla in large bowl. Stir in remaining chips and walnuts. Spread evenly over hot baked crust.

3. Bake 25 minutes or until golden brown. Cool completely in pan on wire rack. Cut into 2- or 2½-inch squares; cut squares diagonally into triangles. Sift powdered sugar over top, if desired.   *Makes 24 or 40 triangles*

Tip: To sprinkle powdered sugar over brownies, bars, cupcakes or other desserts, place sugar in a wire mesh strainer. Hold over top of desserts and gently tap sides of strainer.

Prep Time: 20 minutes
Bake Time: 40 minutes
Cool Time: 2 hours

Peanut Butter Chip Triangles

Pumpkin Harvest Bars

1¾ cups all-purpose flour
2 teaspoons baking powder
1 teaspoon grated orange peel
1 teaspoon ground cinnamon
½ teaspoon salt
½ teaspoon ground nutmeg
¼ teaspoon ground ginger
¼ teaspoon ground cloves
¾ cup sugar
½ cup MOTT'S® Natural Apple Sauce
½ cup solid-pack pumpkin
1 whole egg
1 egg white
2 tablespoons vegetable oil
½ cup raisins

1. Preheat oven to 350°F. Spray 13×9-inch baking pan with nonstick cooking spray.

2. In small bowl, combine flour, baking powder, orange peel, cinnamon, salt, nutmeg, ginger and cloves.

3. In large bowl, combine sugar, apple sauce, pumpkin, whole egg, egg white and oil.

4. Add flour mixture to apple sauce mixture; stir until well blended. Stir in raisins. Spread batter into prepared pan.

5. Bake 25 to 30 minutes or until toothpick inserted in center comes out clean. Cool on wire rack 15 minutes; cut into 16 bars. *Makes 16 servings*

Pumpkin Harvest Bars

Peanut Butter Marshmallow Bars

½ **Butter Flavored CRISCO® Stick or ½ cup Butter Flavor CRISCO®**
all-vegetable shortening, plus additional for greasing
½ **cup JIF® Extra Crunchy Peanut Butter**
¼ **cup firmly packed light brown sugar**
¼ **cup granulated sugar**
1 **egg**
1¼ **cups all-purpose flour**
1 **teaspoon baking powder**
¼ **teaspoon salt**
½ **cup JIF® Creamy Peanut Butter**
4 **cups miniature marshmallows**
½ **cup chocolate flavored syrup**

Preheat oven to 350°F. Grease 13×9×2-inch glass baking dish with shortening.

For cookie base, combine ½ cup shortening, crunchy peanut butter, brown sugar, granulated sugar and egg in large bowl. Beat at medium speed of electric mixer until well blended.

Combine flour, baking powder and salt. Add gradually to creamed mixture at low speed. Beat until well blended. Cover and refrigerate 15 minutes. Press chilled cookie base into prepared dish. Bake for 20 minutes or until light brown. Do not overbake. Cool 2 to 3 minutes.

For topping, place creamy peanut butter in microwave-safe measuring cup. Microwave at HIGH for 1 minute. Pour over baked surface. Spread to cover. Top with marshmallows. Drizzle chocolate syrup over marshmallows. Return to oven. Bake 5 minutes or until marshmallows are light brown. Do not overbake. Loosen from sides of dish with knife. Remove dish to cooling rack. Cool completely. Cut with sharp greased knife into bars about 2×2 inches. *Makes 2 dozen bars*

Peanut Butter Marshmallow Bars

Cappuccino Crunch Bars

1¾ cups all-purpose flour, sifted
1 teaspoon baking soda
1 teaspoon salt
½ teaspoon ground cinnamon
1 cup (2 sticks) butter, softened
1½ cups firmly packed brown sugar
½ cup granulated sugar
2 eggs
2 teaspoons instant coffee granules or espresso powder, dissolved
in 1 tablespoon hot water and cooled to room temperature
2 teaspoons vanilla
1 teaspoon grated orange peel (optional)
1 cup white chocolate chips
1 cup chocolate-covered toffee bits

1. Preheat oven to 350°F. Grease 13×9-inch baking pan. Combine flour, baking soda, salt and cinnamon in large bowl; set aside.

2. Beat butter and sugars with electric mixer at medium speed until fluffy. Add eggs, one at a time, beating well after each addition. Add coffee mixture, vanilla and orange peel, if desired; beat well. Stir in chocolate chips and toffee bits.

3. Pour batter evenly into prepared pan. Bake 25 to 35 minutes or until golden brown. Cool completely in pan on wire rack; cut into bars.   *Makes about 30 bars*

Cappuccino Crunch Bars

Creamy Lemon Bars

1 package (2-layer size) lemon cake mix
3 large eggs, divided
½ cup oil
2 packages (8 ounces each) PHILADELPHIA® Cream Cheese, softened
1 container (8 ounces) BREAKSTONE'S® or KNUDSEN® Sour Cream
½ cup granulated sugar
1 teaspoon grated lemon peel
1 tablespoon lemon juice
Powdered sugar

MIX cake mix, 1 of the eggs and oil. Press mixture onto bottom and up sides of lightly greased 15×10×1-inch baking pan. Bake at 350°F for 10 minutes.

MIX cream cheese with electric mixer on medium speed until smooth. Add remaining 2 eggs, sour cream, granulated sugar, lemon peel and juice; mix until blended. Pour batter into crust.

BAKE at 350°F for 30 to 35 minutes or until filling is just set in center and edges are light golden brown. Cool. Sprinkle with powdered sugar. Cut into bars.

Makes 2 dozen

Storage Know-How: Store leftover bars in tightly covered container in refrigerator.

Prep Time: 15 minutes
Bake Time: 35 minutes

Creamy Lemon Bars

Apple Golden Raisin Cheesecake Bars

1½ cups rolled oats
¾ cup all-purpose flour
½ cup firmly packed light brown sugar
¾ cup plus 2 tablespoons granulated sugar, divided
¾ Butter Flavor CRISCO® Stick or ¾ cup Butter Flavor CRISCO®
all-vegetable shortening
2 (8-ounce) packages cream cheese, softened
2 large eggs
1 teaspoon vanilla
1 cup chopped Granny Smith apples
½ cup golden raisins
1 teaspoon almond extract
½ teaspoon ground cinnamon
¼ teaspoon ground nutmeg
¼ teaspoon ground allspice

1. Heat oven to 350°F.

2. Combine oats, flour, brown sugar and ¼ cup granulated sugar in large bowl; mix well. Cut in ¾ cup shortening with fork until crumbs form. Reserve 1 cup mixture.

3. Spray 13×9-inch baking pan with CRISCO® No-Stick Cooking Spray. Press remaining mixture onto bottom of prepared pan. Bake at 350°F for 12 to 15 minutes or until mixture is set. *Do not brown.* Place on cooling rack.

4. Combine cream cheese, eggs, ½ cup granulated sugar and vanilla in large bowl. Beat at medium speed with electric mixer until well blended. Spread evenly over crust.

5. Combine apples and raisins in medium bowl. Add almond extract; stir. Add remaining 2 tablespoons granulated sugar, cinnamon, nutmeg and allspice; mix well. Top cream cheese mixture evenly with apple mixture; sprinkle reserved oat mixture evenly over top. Bake at 350°F for 20 to 25 minutes or until top is golden. Place on cooling rack; cool completely. Cut into bars.   *Makes 18 bars*

Kitchen Hint: Forgot to take the cream cheese out to soften? Don't worry, simply remove it from the wrapper and place it in a medium microwave-safe bowl. Microwave on MEDIUM (50% power) 15 to 20 seconds or until slightly softened.

Apple Golden Raisin Cheesecake Bars

Chocolate Chip Candy Cookie Bars

1⅔ cups all-purpose flour
2 tablespoons plus 1½ cups sugar, divided
¾ teaspoon baking powder
1 cup (2 sticks) cold butter or margarine, divided
1 egg, slightly beaten
½ cup plus 2 tablespoons (5-ounce can) evaporated milk, divided
2 cups (12-ounce package) HERSHEY'S Semi-Sweet Chocolate Chips, divided
½ cup light corn syrup
1½ cups sliced almonds

1. Heat oven to 375°F.

2. Stir together flour, 2 tablespoons sugar and baking powder in medium bowl; using pastry blender, cut in ½ cup butter until mixture forms coarse crumbs. Stir in egg and 2 tablespoons evaporated milk; stir until mixture holds together in ball shape. Press onto bottom and ¼ inch up sides of 15½×10½×1-inch jelly-roll pan.

3. Bake 8 to 10 minutes or until lightly browned; remove from oven, leaving oven on. Sprinkle 1½ cups chocolate chips evenly over crust; do not disturb chips.

4. Place remaining 1½ cups sugar, remaining ½ cup butter, remaining ½ cup evaporated milk and corn syrup in 3-quart saucepan. Cook over medium heat, stirring constantly, until mixture boils; stir in almonds. Continue cooking and stirring to 240°F on candy thermometer (soft-ball stage) or until small amount of mixture, when dropped into very cold water, forms a soft ball which flattens when removed from water. (Bulb of candy thermometer should not rest on bottom of saucepan.) Remove from heat. Immediately spoon almond mixture evenly over chips and crust; do not spread.

5. Bake 10 to 15 minutes or just until almond mixture is golden brown. Remove from oven; cool 5 minutes. Sprinkle remaining ½ cup chips over top; cool completely. Cut into bars. *Makes about 48 bars*

Chocolate Chip Candy Cookie Bars

Golden Peanut Butter Bars

2 cups all-purpose flour
¾ cup firmly packed light brown sugar
1 egg, beaten
½ cup (1 stick) cold butter or margarine
1 cup finely chopped peanuts
1 (14-ounce) can EAGLE BRAND® Sweetened Condensed Milk
   (NOT evaporated milk)
½ cup peanut butter
1 teaspoon vanilla extract

1. Preheat oven to 350°F. In large mixing bowl, combine flour, brown sugar and egg; cut in cold butter until crumbly. Stir in peanuts. Reserve 2 cups crumb mixture. Press remaining mixture on bottom of 13×9-inch baking pan.

2. Bake 15 minutes or until lightly browned.

3. Meanwhile, in another large mixing bowl, beat Eagle Brand, peanut butter and vanilla. Spread over prepared crust; top with reserved crumb mixture.

4. Bake an additional 25 minutes or until lightly browned. Cool. Cut into bars. Store covered at room temperature. *Makes 24 to 36 bars*

Prep Time: 20 minutes
Bake Time: 40 minutes

Golden Peanut Butter Bars

Lemon Raspberry Cheesecake Bars

CRUST
   ¾ **Butter Flavor CRISCO® Stick or ¾ cup Butter Flavor CRISCO®**
      All-Vegetable Shortening, plus additional for greasing pan
   ½ **cup firmly packed brown sugar**
1 ¼ **cups all-purpose flour**
   1 **cup uncooked oats**
   ¼ **teaspoon salt**

FILLING
   ½ **cup SMUCKER'S® Red Raspberry Jam**
   2 **(8-ounce) packages cream cheese, softened**
   ¾ **cup granulated sugar**
   2 **tablespoons all-purpose flour**
   2 **eggs**
   2 **teaspoons grated lemon peel**
   3 **tablespoons lemon juice**

Preheat oven to 350°F. Grease 13×9×2-inch baking pan with shortening.

For crust, combine ¾ cup shortening and brown sugar. Beat at medium speed with electric mixer until well blended. Add 1¼ cups flour, oats and salt gradually at low speed. Mix until well blended. Press onto bottom of prepared pan.

Bake for 20 minutes or until lightly browned

For filling, spoon jam immediately on hot crust. Spread carefully to cover.

Combine cream cheese, granulated sugar and 2 tablespoons flour in large bowl. Beat at low speed until well blended. Add eggs. Mix well. Add lemon peel and lemon juice. Beat until smooth. Pour over raspberry layer.

Bake for 25 minutes or until set. Remove pan to cooling rack and cool to room temperature. Cut into bars about 2×1½ inches. Cover and refrigerate.

Makes 3 dozen bars

Lemon Raspberry Cheesecake Bars

Cocoa Bottom Banana Pecan Bars

   1 cup sugar
   ½ cup (1 stick) butter, softened
   1 egg
   1 teaspoon vanilla
   5 ripe bananas, mashed
1 ½ cups all-purpose flour
   1 teaspoon baking powder
   1 teaspoon baking soda
   ½ teaspoon salt
   ½ cup chopped pecans
   ¼ cup cocoa

Preheat oven to 350°F. Grease 13×9-inch pan. Beat sugar and butter in large bowl with electric mixer until creamy. Add egg and vanilla; beat until well combined. Beat in bananas. Combine flour, baking powder, baking soda and salt. Add to banana mixture; mix well. Sir in pecans. Divide batter in half and add cocoa to one half. Spread cocoa batter into prepared pan. Spread remaining batter over cocoa batter; swirl with knife. Bake 30 to 35 minutes or until edges are lightly browned and toothpick inserted into center comes out clean.   *Makes 12 to 14 servings*

Easy Cookie Bars

   ½ cup (1 stick) butter or margarine, melted
1 ½ cups HONEY MAID® Graham Cracker Crumbs
1 ⅓ cups BAKER'S® ANGEL FLAKE® Coconut
   1 cup BAKER'S® Semi-Sweet Chocolate Chunks
   1 cup chopped PLANTERS® Pecans
   1 can (14 ounces) sweetened condensed milk

MIX butter and graham cracker crumbs in medium bowl. Press onto bottom of greased foil-lined 13×9-inch baking pan.

SPRINKLE with coconut, chocolate chunks and nuts. Pour condensed milk over top.

BAKE at 350°F for 25 to 30 minutes or until golden brown. Cool completely in pan on wire rack. Lift out of pan onto cutting board.   *Makes 3 dozen bars*

Tip: If baking in a 13×9-inch glass baking dish, reduce oven temperature to 325°F.

Cocoa Bottom Banana Pecan Bars

Chunky Pecan Pie Bars

Crust
 1½ **cups all-purpose flour**
  ½ **cup (1 stick) butter or margarine, softened**
  ¼ **cup packed brown sugar**

Filling
  3 **large eggs**
  ¾ **cup corn syrup**
  ¾ **cup granulated sugar**
  2 **tablespoons butter or margarine, melted**
  1 **teaspoon vanilla extract**
 1¾ **cups (11.5-ounce package) NESTLÉ® TOLL HOUSE®**
   Semi-Sweet Chocolate Chunks
 1½ **cups coarsely chopped pecans**

PREHEAT oven to 350°F. Grease 13×9-inch baking pan.

For Crust

BEAT flour, butter and brown sugar in small mixer bowl until crumbly. Press into prepared baking pan.

BAKE for 12 to 15 minutes or until lightly browned.

For Filling

BEAT eggs, corn syrup, granulated sugar, butter and vanilla extract in medium bowl with wire whisk. Stir in chunks and nuts. Pour evenly over baked crust.

BAKE for 25 to 30 minutes or until set. Cool completely in pan on wire rack. Cut into bars. *Makes 2 to 3 dozen bars*

Chunky Pecan Pie Bars

Blueberry Cheesecake Bars

**1 package DUNCAN HINES® Bakery-Style Blueberry Streusel
   Muffin Mix**
¼ cup cold butter or margarine
⅓ cup finely chopped pecans
1 package (8 ounces) cream cheese, softened
½ cup sugar
1 egg
3 tablespoons lemon juice
1 teaspoon grated lemon peel

1. Preheat oven to 350°F. Grease 9-inch square baking pan.

2. Rinse blueberries from Mix with cold water and drain; set aside.

3. Place muffin mix in medium bowl; cut in butter with pastry blender or two knives. Stir in pecans. Press into bottom of prepared pan. Bake at 350°F for 15 minutes or until set.

4. Combine cream cheese and sugar in medium bowl. Beat until smooth. Add egg, lemon juice and lemon peel. Beat well. Spread over baked crust. Sprinkle with blueberries. Sprinkle topping packet from Mix over blueberries. Return to oven. Bake at 350°F for 35 to 40 minutes or until filling is set. Cool completely. Refrigerate until ready to serve. Cut into bars. *Makes about 16 bars*

Blueberry Cheesecake Bars

Praline Bars

¾ cup (1½ sticks) butter or margarine, softened
1 cup sugar, divided
1 teaspoon vanilla, divided
1½ cups flour
2 packages (8 ounces each) PHILADELPHIA® Cream Cheese, softened
2 eggs
½ cup almond brickle chips
3 tablespoons caramel-flavored dessert topping

MIX butter, ½ cup of the sugar and ½ teaspoon of the vanilla with electric mixer on medium speed until light and fluffy. Gradually add flour, mixing on low speed until blended. Press onto bottom of 13×9-inch baking pan. Bake at 350°F for 20 to 23 minutes or until lightly browned.

MIX cream cheese, remaining ½ cup sugar and remaining ½ teaspoon vanilla with electric mixer on medium speed until well blended. Add eggs; mix well. Blend in chips. Pour over crust. Drop teaspoonfuls of caramel topping over cream cheese mixture. Cut through batter with knife several times for marble effect.

BAKE at 350°F for 30 minutes. Cool in pan on wire rack. Refrigerate. Cut into bars.

Makes 24 bars

Take a Shortcut: To quickly soften 8 ounces cream cheese, microwave on HIGH for 10 to 15 seconds.

Prep Time: 30 minutes
Bake Time: 1 hour 23 minutes

Praline Bars

brownies & blondies

Layers of Love Chocolate Brownies

¾ cup all-purpose flour
¾ cup **NESTLÉ® TOLL HOUSE® Baking Cocoa**
¼ teaspoon salt
½ cup (1 stick) butter, cut in pieces
½ cup granulated sugar
½ cup packed brown sugar
3 large eggs, *divided*
2 teaspoons vanilla extract
1 cup chopped pecans
¾ cup **NESTLÉ® TOLL HOUSE® Premier White Morsels**
½ cup caramel ice cream topping
¾ cup **NESTLÉ® TOLL HOUSE® Semi-Sweet Chocolate Morsels**

PREHEAT oven to 350°F. Grease 8-inch-square baking pan.

COMBINE flour, cocoa and salt in small bowl. Beat butter, granulated sugar and brown sugar in large mixer bowl until creamy. Add *2 eggs,* one at a time, beating well after each addition. Add vanilla extract; mix well. Gradually beat in flour mixture. Reserve *¾ cup* batter. Spread *remaining* batter into prepared baking pan. Sprinkle pecans and white morsels over batter. Drizzle caramel topping over top. Beat *remaining* egg and *reserved* batter in same large bowl until light in color. Stir in semi-sweet morsels. Spread evenly over caramel topping.

BAKE for 30 to 35 minutes or until center is set. Cool completely in pan on wire rack. Cut into squares. *Makes 16 brownies*

Layers of Love Chocolate Brownies

Dulce de Leche Blondies

2 cups all-purpose flour
1 teaspoon baking soda
1 teaspoon salt
1 cup (2 sticks) unsalted butter, softened
1 cup firmly packed brown sugar
2 eggs
1 ½ teaspoons vanilla
1 package (14 ounces) caramels
½ cup evaporated milk

Preheat oven to 350°F. Grease 13×9-inch baking pan. Sift flour, baking soda and salt. Beat butter and sugar until creamy. Add eggs and vanilla; beat until smooth. Gradually stir in flour mixture. Spread ½ to ⅔ of mixture in prepared pan. Bake 7 to 8 minutes. Let cool 5 minutes on wire rack. Meanwhile, melt caramels in evaporated milk in nonstick saucepan over very low heat. Reserve 2 tablespoons; pour remaining caramel over baked layer. Drop dollops of remaining dough over caramel layer; swirl slightly with knife. Bake 25 minutes or until golden brown. Cool in pan on wire rack. When completely cooled, cut into 1-inch squares. Reheat reserved caramel, if necessary; drizzle over blondies.   *Makes about 3 dozen blondies*

No-Bake Fudgy Brownies

1 (14-ounce) can EAGLE BRAND® Sweetened Condensed Milk
**   (NOT evaporated milk)**
2 (1-ounce) squares unsweetened chocolate, cut up
1 teaspoon vanilla extract
2 cups plus 2 tablespoons packaged chocolate cookie crumbs, divided
¼ cup miniature candy-coated milk chocolate pieces or chopped nuts

1. Grease 8-inch square baking pan or line with foil. In heavy saucepan over low heat, cook and stir Eagle Brand and chocolate just until boiling. Reduce heat; cook and stir 2 to 3 minutes more or until mixture thickens. Remove from heat. Stir in vanilla.

2. Stir in 2 cups cookie crumbs. Spread evenly in prepared pan. Sprinkle with remaining crumbs and chocolate pieces or nuts; press down gently with back of spoon.

3. Cover and chill 4 hours or until firm. Cut into squares. Store covered in refrigerator.   *Makes 24 to 36 bars*

Dulce de Leche Blondies

Hershey's Best Brownies

1 cup (2 sticks) butter or margarine
2 cups sugar
2 teaspoons vanilla extract
4 eggs
¾ cup HERSHEY'S Cocoa or HERSHEY'S Dutch Processed Cocoa
1 cup all-purpose flour
½ teaspoon baking powder
¼ teaspoon salt
1 cup chopped nuts (optional)

1. Heat oven to 350°F. Grease 13×9×2-inch baking pan.

2. Place butter in large microwave-safe bowl. Microwave at HIGH (100%) 2 to 2½ minutes or until melted. Stir in sugar and vanilla. Add eggs, one at a time, beating well with spoon after each addition. Add cocoa; beat until well blended. Add flour, baking powder and salt; beat well. Stir in nuts, if desired. Pour batter into prepared pan.

3. Bake 30 to 35 minutes or until brownies begin to pull away from sides of pan. Cool completely in pan on wire rack. Cut into bars.   *Makes about 36 brownies*

Creamy Cappuccino Brownies

1 package (21 to 24 ounces) brownie mix
1 tablespoon coffee crystals *or* 1 teaspoon espresso powder
2 tablespoons warm water
1 cup (8 ounces) Wisconsin Mascarpone cheese
3 tablespoons granulated sugar
1 egg
Powdered sugar

Grease bottom of 13×9-inch baking pan. Prepare brownie mix according to package directions. Pour half of batter into prepared pan. Dissolve coffee crystals in water; add Mascarpone, granulated sugar and egg. Blend until smooth. Drop by spoonfuls over brownie batter; top with remaining brownie batter. With knife, swirl cheese mixture through brownies creating marbled effect. Bake at 375°F 30 to 35 minutes or until toothpick inserted in center comes out clean. Sprinkle with powdered sugar.
Makes 2 dozen brownies

*Favorite recipe from **Wisconsin Milk Marketing Board***

Hershey's Best Brownies

Bittersweet Pecan Brownies with Caramel Sauce

Brownies
- ¾ **cup all-purpose flour**
- ¼ **teaspoon baking soda**
- 4 **squares (1 ounce each) bittersweet or unsweetened chocolate, coarsely chopped**
- ½ **cup (1 stick) plus 2 tablespoons I CAN'T BELIEVE IT'S NOT BUTTER!® Spread**
- ¾ **cup granulated sugar**
- 2 **eggs**
- ½ **cup chopped pecans**

Caramel Sauce
- ¾ **cup firmly packed light brown sugar**
- 6 **tablespoons I CAN'T BELIEVE IT'S NOT BUTTER!® Spread**
- ⅓ **cup whipping or heavy cream**
- ½ **teaspoon apple cider vinegar or fresh lemon juice**

For brownies, preheat oven to 325°F. Line 8-inch square baking pan with aluminum foil, then grease and flour foil; set aside.

In small bowl, combine flour and baking soda; set aside.

In medium microwave-safe bowl, microwave chocolate and I Can't Believe It's Not Butter!® Spread at HIGH (100%) 1 minute or until chocolate is melted; stir until smooth. With wooden spoon, beat in granulated sugar, then eggs. Beat in flour mixture. Evenly spread into prepared pan; sprinkle with pecans.

Bake 31 minutes or until toothpick inserted in center comes out clean. On wire rack, cool completely. To remove brownies, lift edges of foil. Cut brownies into 4 squares, then cut each square into 2 triangles.

For caramel sauce, in medium saucepan, bring brown sugar, I Can't Believe It's Not Butter! Spread and cream just to a boil over high heat, stirring frequently. Cook 3 minutes. Stir in vinegar. To serve, pour caramel sauce around brownie and top, if desired, with vanilla or caramel ice cream.   *Makes 8 servings*

Bittersweet Pecan Brownies with Caramel Sauce

Festive Fruited White Chip Blondies

½ cup (1 stick) butter or margarine
1⅔ cups (10-ounce package) HERSHEY'S Premier White Chips, divided
  2 eggs
¼ cup granulated sugar
1¼ cups all-purpose flour
⅓ cup orange juice
¾ cup cranberries, chopped
¼ cup chopped dried apricots
½ cup coarsely chopped nuts
¼ cup packed light brown sugar

1. Heat oven to 325°F. Grease and flour 9-inch square baking pan.

2. Melt butter in medium saucepan; stir in 1 cup white chips. Beat eggs in large bowl until foamy. Add granulated sugar; beat until thick and pale yellow in color. Add flour, orange juice and white chip mixture; beat just until combined. Spread one-half of batter, about 1¼ cups, into prepared pan.

3. Bake 15 minutes or until edges are lightly browned; remove from oven.

4. Stir cranberries, apricots and remaining ⅔ cup white chips into remaining one-half of batter; spread over top of hot baked mixture. Stir together nuts and brown sugar; sprinkle over top.

5. Bake 25 to 30 minutes or until edges are lightly browned. Cool completely in pan on wire rack. Cut into bars.   *Makes about 16 bars*

Festive Fruited White Chip Blondies

Easy Double Chocolate Chip Brownies

    2 cups (12-ounce package) NESTLÉ® TOLL HOUSE®
        Semi-Sweet Chocolate Morsels, *divided*
  ½ cup (1 stick) butter or margarine, cut into pieces
    3 large eggs
1 ¼ cups all-purpose flour
    1 cup granulated sugar
    1 teaspoon vanilla extract
  ¼ teaspoon baking soda
  ½ cup chopped nuts

PREHEAT oven to 350°F. Grease 13×9-inch baking pan.

MELT *1 cup* morsels and butter in large, *heavy-duty* saucepan over low heat; stir until smooth. Remove from heat. Stir in eggs. Stir in flour, sugar, vanilla extract and baking soda. Stir in *remaining* morsels and nuts. Spread into prepared baking pan.

BAKE for 18 to 22 minutes or until wooden pick inserted in center comes out slightly sticky. Cool completely in pan on wire rack.   *Makes 2 dozen brownies*

Nuggets o' Gold Brownies

    3 ounces unsweetened baking chocolate
¼ cup WESSON® Vegetable Oil
  2 eggs
  1 cup sugar
  1 teaspoon vanilla extract
¼ teaspoon salt
  ½ cup all-purpose flour
  1 (3.8-ounce) BUTTERFINGER® Candy Bar, coarsely chopped

In microwave-safe measuring cup, heat chocolate 2 minutes on HIGH in microwave oven. Stir and continue heating in 30-second intervals until chocolate is completely melted. Stir in oil and set aside to cool. In mixing bowl, beat eggs until foamy. Whisk in sugar, then add vanilla and salt. Stir in chocolate mixture, then mix in flour until all ingredients are moistened. Gently fold in candy. Pour batter into greased 9-inch baking pan and bake at 350°F for 25 to 30 minutes or until edges begin to pull away from sides of pan. Cool before cutting.   *Makes 20 brownies*

Easy Double Chocolate Chip Brownies

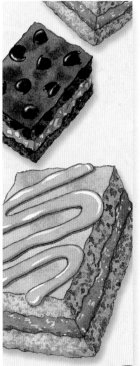

Three Great Tastes Blond Brownies

2 cups packed light brown sugar
1 cup (2 sticks) butter or margarine, melted
2 eggs
2 teaspoons vanilla extract
2 cups all-purpose flour
1 teaspoon salt
⅔ cup (of each) HERSHEY'S Semi-Sweet Chocolate Chips, REESE'S®
    Peanut Butter Chips, and HERSHEY'S Premier White Chips
    Chocolate Chip Drizzle (recipe follows)

1. Heat oven to 350°F. Grease 15½×10½×1-inch jelly-roll pan.

2. Stir together brown sugar and butter in large bowl; beat in eggs and vanilla until smooth. Add flour and salt, beating just until blended; stir in chocolate, peanut butter and white chips. Spread batter into prepared pan.

3. Bake 25 to 30 minutes or until wooden pick inserted in center comes out clean. Cool completely in pan on wire rack. Cut into bars. With tines of fork, drizzle Chocolate Chip Drizzle randomly over bars.   *Makes about 72 bars*

Chocolate Chip Drizzle: Place ¼ cup HERSHEY'S Semi-Sweet Chocolate Chips and ¼ teaspoon shortening (do not use butter, margarine, spread or oil) in small microwave-safe bowl. Microwave at HIGH (100%) 30 seconds to 1 minute; stir until chips are melted and mixture is smooth.

Three Great Tastes Blond Brownies

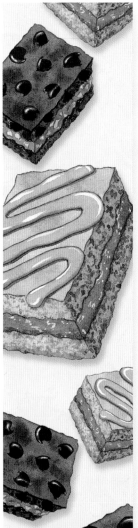

Chunky Caramel Nut Brownies

4 squares (1 ounce each) unsweetened chocolate
¾ cup (1½ sticks) butter
2 cups sugar
4 eggs
1 cup all-purpose flour
1 package (14 ounces) caramels
¼ cup heavy cream
2 cups pecan halves or coarsely chopped pecans, divided
1 package (12 ounces) chocolate chunks or chips

1. Preheat oven to 350°F. Grease 13×9-inch baking pan; set aside.

2. Place chocolate and butter in large microwavable bowl. Microwave at HIGH 1½ to 2 minutes or until chocolate is melted and mixture is smooth when stirred. Stir in sugar until well blended. Beat in eggs, 1 at a time. Stir in flour until well blended. Spread half of batter in prepared pan.

3. Bake 20 minutes. Meanwhile, combine caramels and cream in medium microwavable bowl. Microwave at HIGH 1½ to 2 minutes or until caramels begin to melt; stir until mixture is smooth. Stir in 1 cup pecan halves.

4. Spread caramel mixture over partially baked brownie. Sprinkle with half of chocolate chunks. Pour remaining brownie batter over top; sprinkle with remaining 1 cup pecan halves and chocolate chunks. Bake 25 to 30 minutes more or until set. Cool in pan on wire rack. *Makes 24 brownies*

Chunky Caramel Nut Brownies

Almond Brownies

    ½ cup (1 stick) butter
    2 squares (1 ounce each) unsweetened baking chocolate
    2 large eggs
    1 cup firmly packed light brown sugar
    ¼ teaspoon almond extract
    ½ cup all-purpose flour
1½ cups "M&M's"® Chocolate Mini Baking Bits, divided
    ½ cup slivered almonds, toasted and divided
    Chocolate Glaze (recipe follows)

Preheat oven to 350°F. Grease and flour 8×8×2-inch baking pan; set aside. In small saucepan melt butter and chocolate over low heat; stir to blend. Remove from heat; let cool. In medium bowl beat eggs and brown sugar until well blended; stir in chocolate mixture and almond extract. Add flour. Stir in 1 cup "M&M's"® Chocolate Mini Baking Bits and ¼ cup almonds. Spread batter evenly in prepared pan. Bake 25 to 28 minutes or until firm in center. Cool completely on wire rack. Prepare Chocolate Glaze. Spread over brownies; decorate with remaining ½ cup "M&M's"® Chocolate Mini Baking Bits and remaining ¼ cup almonds. Cut into bars. Store in tightly covered container. *Makes 16 brownies*

Chocolate Glaze: In small saucepan over low heat combine 4 teaspoons water and 1 tablespoon butter until it comes to a boil. Stir in 4 teaspoons unsweetened cocoa powder. Gradually stir in ½ cup powdered sugar until smooth. Remove from heat; stir in ¼ teaspoon vanilla extract. Let glaze cool slightly.

Almond Brownies

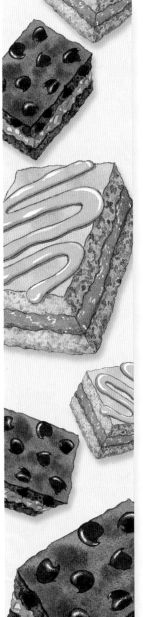

Chewy Macadamia Nut Blondies

**¾ Butter Flavor CRISCO® Stick or ¾ cup Butter Flavor CRISCO®
all-vegetable shortening**
1 cup firmly packed light brown sugar
1 egg
1 teaspoon vanilla
1 teaspoon almond extract
1 cup all-purpose flour
½ teaspoon baking soda
⅛ teaspoon salt
6 ounces white chocolate chips
1 cup chopped macadamia nuts

1. Heat oven to 325°F. Place wire rack on countertop for cooling bars.

2. Combine ¾ cup shortening and sugar in large bowl. Beat at medium speed of electric mixer until well blended. Beat in egg, vanilla and almond extract until well blended.

3. Combine flour, baking soda and salt in small bowl. Add to creamed mixture until just incorporated. *Do not overmix.* Fold in white chocolate chips and nuts until just blended.

4. Spray 9-inch square baking pan with CRISCO® No-Stick Cooking Spray. Pour batter into prepared pan. Bake at 325°F for 25 to 30 minutes or until toothpick inserted in center comes out almost dry and top is golden. *Do not overbake or overbrown.*

5. Cool completely in pan on wire rack. Cut into bars.   *Makes about 16 bars*

German's® Chocolate Brownies

1 package (4 ounces) BAKER'S® GERMAN'S® Sweet Chocolate
¼ cup (½ stick) butter or margarine
¾ cup sugar
2 eggs
1 teaspoon vanilla
½ cup flour
½ cup chopped PLANTERS® Pecans

MICROWAVE chocolate and butter in large microwavable bowl on HIGH 2 minutes or until butter is melted. Stir until chocolate is completely melted.

ADD sugar to chocolate mixture. Stir until well blended. Mix in eggs and vanilla. Stir in flour and pecans until well blended. Spread in greased foil-lined 8-inch square baking pan.

BAKE at 350°F for 25 minutes or until toothpick inserted in center comes out with fudgy crumbs. DO NOT OVERBAKE. Cool in pan. Run knife around edges of pan to loosen brownies from sides. Lift from pan using foil as handles. Cut into squares.

Makes 16 brownies

Tip: If baking in 8-inch square glass baking dish, reduce oven temperature to 325°F.

Coconut Topped Brownies: Increase pecans to 1 cup. Prepare brownie batter as directed, using ½ cup of the pecans. Spread in prepared pan as directed. Mix 1⅓ cups (3½ ounces) BAKER'S® ANGEL FLAKE® Coconut, remaining ½ cup pecans and ¼ cup firmly packed brown sugar in small bowl. Stir in ¼ cup milk until well blended. Spoon mixture evenly over brownie batter. Bake at 350°F for 40 minutes or until toothpick inserted in center comes out with fudgy crumbs.

Prep Time: 15 minutes
Total Time: 40 minutes

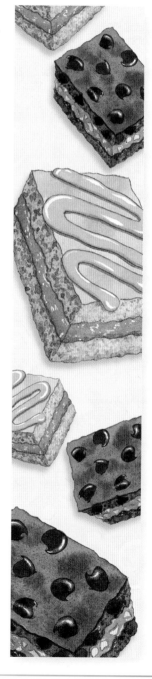

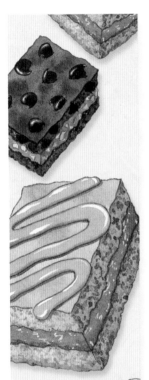

Rocky Road Brownies

1¼ cups miniature marshmallows
1 cup HERSHEY'S Semi-Sweet Chocolate Chips
½ cup chopped nuts
½ cup (1 stick) butter or margarine
1 cup sugar
1 teaspoon vanilla extract
2 eggs
½ cup all-purpose flour
⅓ cup HERSHEY'S Cocoa
½ teaspoon baking powder
½ teaspoon salt

1. Heat oven to 350°F. Grease 9-inch square baking pan.

2. Stir together marshmallows, chocolate chips and nuts; set aside. Place butter in large microwave-safe bowl. Microwave at HIGH (100% power) 1 to 1½ minutes or until melted. Add sugar, vanilla and eggs, beating with spoon until well blended. Add flour, cocoa, baking powder and salt; blend well. Spread batter in prepared pan.

3. Bake 22 minutes. Sprinkle chocolate chip mixture over top. Continue baking 5 minutes or until marshmallows have softened and puffed slightly. Cool completely. With wet knife, cut into squares. *Makes about 20 brownies*

Rocky Road Brownies

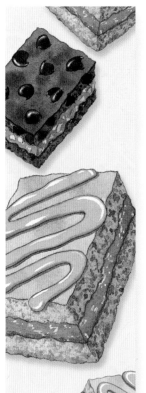

Coconutty "M&M's"® Brownies

    6 squares (1 ounce each) semi-sweet chocolate
    ¾ cup granulated sugar
    ½ cup (1 stick) butter
    2 large eggs
    1 tablespoon vegetable oil
    1 teaspoon vanilla extract
1¼ cups all-purpose flour
    3 tablespoons unsweetened cocoa powder
    1 teaspoon baking powder
    ½ teaspoon salt
1½ cups "M&M's"® Chocolate Mini Baking Bits, divided
        Coconut Topping (recipe follows)

Preheat oven to 350°F. Lightly grease 8×8×2-inch baking pan. In small saucepan combine chocolate, sugar and butter over low heat; stir constantly until chocolate is melted. Remove from heat; let cool slightly. In large bowl beat eggs, oil and vanilla; stir in chocolate mixture until well blended. In medium bowl combine flour, cocoa powder, baking powder and salt; add to chocolate mixture. Stir in 1 cup "M&M's"® Chocolate Mini Baking Bits. Spread batter evenly in prepared pan. Bake 35 to 40 minutes or until toothpick inserted in center comes out clean. Cool completely on wire rack. Prepare Coconut Topping. Spread over brownies; sprinkle with remaining ½ cup "M&M's"® Chocolate Mini Baking Bits. Cut into bars. Store in tightly covered container. *Makes 16 brownies*

Coconut Topping

    ½ cup (1 stick) butter
    ⅓ cup firmly packed light brown sugar
    ⅓ cup light corn syrup
    1 cup sweetened shredded coconut, toasted*
    ¾ cup chopped pecans
    1 teaspoon vanilla extract

*To toast coconut, spread evenly on cookie sheet. Toast in preheated 350°F oven 7 to 8 minutes or until golden brown, stirring occasionally.

In large saucepan melt butter over medium heat. Add brown sugar and corn syrup; stir constantly until thick and bubbly. Remove from heat; stir in remaining ingredients.

Coconutty "M&M's"® Brownies

chocolate indulgence

Malted Milk Cookies

1 cup (2 sticks) butter
¾ cup granulated sugar
¾ cup packed brown sugar
1 teaspoon baking soda
2 eggs
2 squares (1 ounce each) unsweetened chocolate, melted and cooled to room temperature
1 teaspoon vanilla
2¼ cups all-purpose flour
½ cup instant malted milk powder
1 cup chopped malted milk balls

1. Preheat oven to 375°F.

2. Beat butter 30 seconds with electric mixer at medium speed. Add sugars and baking soda; beat until blended. Beat in eggs, chocolate and vanilla until well blended.

3. Beat in as much flour as possible with mixer. Using spoon, stir in any remaining flour and malted milk powder. Stir in malted milk balls.

4. Drop dough by rounded teaspoonfuls 2½ inches apart onto ungreased cookie sheets. Bake about 10 minutes or until edges are firm. Cool on cookie sheets 1 minute. Remove to wire racks; cool completely.   *Makes about 3 dozen cookies*

Malted Milk Cookies

Chocolate Crackletops

2 cups all-purpose flour
2 teaspoons baking powder
2 cups granulated sugar
½ cup (1 stick) butter or margarine
4 squares (1 ounce each) unsweetened baking chocolate, chopped
4 large eggs, lightly beaten
2 teaspoons vanilla extract
1¾ cups "M&M's"® Chocolate Mini Baking Bits
Additional granulated sugar

Combine flour and baking powder; set aside. In 2-quart saucepan over medium heat combine 2 cups sugar, butter and chocolate, stirring until butter and chocolate are melted; remove from heat. Gradually stir in eggs and vanilla. Stir in flour mixture until well blended. Chill mixture 1 hour. Stir in "M&M's"® Chocolate Mini Baking Bits; chill mixture an additional 1 hour.

Preheat oven to 350°F. Line cookie sheets with foil. With sugar-dusted hands, roll dough into 1-inch balls; roll balls in additional granulated sugar. Place about 2 inches apart onto prepared cookie sheets. Bake 10 to 12 minutes. Do not overbake. Cool completely on wire racks. Store in tightly covered container.   *Makes about 5 dozen cookies*

Chocolate Walnut Meringues

3 egg whites
Pinch of salt
¾ cup sugar
½ cup good-quality Dutch-processed cocoa
⅓ cup finely chopped California walnuts

Preheat oven to 350°F. Place egg whites and salt in large mixing bowl. Beat with electric mixer or wire whisk until soft peaks form. Gradually add sugar, beating until stiff peaks form. Sift cocoa over peaks and fold into egg white mixture with walnuts. Spoon mounds about 1 inch in diameter and about 1 inch apart onto parchment-lined baking sheets. Bake 20 minutes or until dry to the touch. Let cool completely before removing from baking sheets. Store in airtight container.   *Makes 48 cookies*

*Favorite recipe from **Walnut Marketing Board***

Chocolate Crackletops

Chocolate White Chocolate Chunk Cookies

2 cups flour
2 teaspoons CALUMET® Baking Powder
¼ teaspoon salt
¾ cup (1½ sticks) butter or margarine, softened
1½ cups firmly packed brown sugar
2 eggs
1 teaspoon vanilla
4 squares BAKER'S® Unsweetened Baking Chocolate, melted, cooled slightly
1 package (12 ounces) BAKER'S® White Chocolate Chunks
1 cup chopped PLANTERS® Pecans (optional)

MIX flour, baking powder and salt; set aside.

BEAT butter and sugar in large bowl with electric mixer on medium speed until light and fluffy. Add eggs and vanilla; mix well. Stir in melted chocolate. Gradually add flour mixture, mixing well after each addition. Stir in chocolate chunks and pecans. Drop by heaping tablespoonfuls onto ungreased cookie sheets.

BAKE at 350°F for 11 to 12 minutes or until cookies feel set to the touch. Cool on cookie sheets 1 minute. Remove to wire racks; cool completely.

Makes about 3½ dozen cookies

Storage Know-How: Store in tightly covered container up to 1 week.

Make-Ahead: After cookies are completely cooled, wrap in plastic wrap and place in an airtight plastic container or zipper-style plastic freezer bag. Cookies can be frozen for up to 1 month. Bring cookies to room temperature before serving.

Prep Time: 15 minutes
Total Time: 27 minutes

Chocolate White Chocolate Chunk Cookies

Chocolate Surprise Cookies

2¾ cups all-purpose flour
¾ cup unsweetened cocoa powder
½ teaspoon baking powder
½ teaspoon baking soda
1 cup (2 sticks) butter, softened
1½ cups packed light brown sugar
½ cup plus 1 tablespoon granulated sugar, divided
2 eggs
1 teaspoon vanilla
1 cup chopped pecans, divided
1 package (9 ounces) caramels coated in milk chocolate
3 squares (1 ounce each) white chocolate, coarsely chopped

Preheat oven to 375°F. Combine flour, cocoa, baking powder and baking soda in medium bowl; set aside.

Beat butter, brown sugar and ½ cup granulated sugar with electric mixer at medium speed until light and fluffy; beat in eggs and vanilla. Gradually add flour mixture and ½ cup pecans; beat well. Cover dough; refrigerate 15 minutes or until firm enough to roll into balls.

Place remaining ½ cup pecans and 1 tablespoon sugar in shallow dish. Roll tablespoonful of dough around 1 caramel candy, covering completely; press one side into nut mixture. Place, nut side up, on ungreased cookie sheet. Repeat with remaining dough and candies, placing 3 inches apart.

Bake 10 to 12 minutes or until set and slightly cracked. Let stand on cookie sheet 2 minutes. Transfer cookies to wire rack; cool completely.

Place white chocolate in small resealable plastic freezer bag; seal bag. Microwave at MEDIUM (50% power) 2 minutes. Turn bag over; microwave 2 to 3 minutes or until melted. Knead bag until chocolate is smooth. Cut off tiny corner of bag; drizzle chocolate onto cookies. Let stand about 30 minutes or until chocolate is set.

Makes about 3½ dozen cookies

Chocolate Surprise Cookies

Mexican Chocolate Macaroons

1 package (8 ounces) semisweet baking chocolate, divided
1¾ cups plus ⅓ cup whole almonds, divided
¾ cup sugar
1 teaspoon ground cinnamon
1 teaspoon vanilla
2 egg whites

Preheat oven to 400°F. Grease cookie sheets. Coarsely chop 5 squares chocolate in food processor. Add 1¾ cups almonds and sugar; process with on/off pulses until mixture is finely ground. Add cinnamon, vanilla and egg whites; process just until mixture forms moist dough. Form dough into 1-inch balls. (Dough will be sticky.) Place about 2 inches apart on prepared cookie sheets. Press whole almond on top of each cookie.

Bake 8 to 10 minutes or just until set. Cool 2 minutes on cookie sheets. Remove to wire racks; cool completely. Melt remaining 3 squares chocolate; drizzle chocolate over cookies.   *Makes 3 dozen cookies*

Reese's® Chewy Chocolate Cookies

2 cups all-purpose flour
¾ cup HERSHEY'S Cocoa
1 teaspoon baking soda
½ teaspoon salt
1¼ cups (2½ sticks) butter or margarine, softened
2 cups sugar
2 eggs
2 teaspoons vanilla extract
1⅔ cups (10-ounce package) REESE'S® Peanut Butter Chips

1. Heat oven to 350°F. Stir together flour, cocoa, baking soda and salt; set aside. Beat butter and sugar in large bowl with mixer until fluffy. Add eggs and vanilla; beat well. Gradually add flour mixture, beating well. Stir in peanut butter chips. Drop by rounded teaspoons onto ungreased cookie sheet.

2. Bake 8 to 9 minutes. (Do not overbake; cookies will be soft. They will puff while baking and flatten while cooling.) Cool slightly; remove from cookie sheet to wire rack. Cool completely.   *Makes about 4½ dozen cookies*

Mexican Chocolate Macaroons

Chocolate Bliss Cookies

1 package (8 squares) BAKER'S® Semi-Sweet Baking Chocolate
¾ cup firmly packed brown sugar
¼ cup (½ stick) butter or margarine
2 eggs
1 teaspoon vanilla
½ cup flour
¼ teaspoon CALUMET® Baking Powder
1 package (8 squares) BAKER'S® Semi-Sweet Baking Chocolate, coarsely chopped, or 1½ cups BAKER'S® Semi-Sweet Chocolate Chunks
2 cups chopped PLANTERS® Walnuts (optional)

MICROWAVE chocolate squares in large microwavable bowl on HIGH 2 minutes. Stir until chocolate is melted. Add sugar, butter, eggs and vanilla; stir with wooden spoon until well blended. Add flour and baking powder; mix well. Stir in chopped chocolate and walnuts. (If omitting nuts, increase flour to ¾ cup to prevent spreading of cookies as they bake.)

DROP rounded tablespoonfuls of dough onto ungreased baking sheets.

BAKE 13 to 14 minutes or until golden brown. Cool 1 minute; remove from baking sheets. Cool completely on wire racks.   *Makes about 2½ dozen cookies*

Bite-Sized Cookies: Drop heaping teaspoonfuls of dough onto ungreased baking sheets. Bake at 350°F for 6 to 7 minutes or until golden brown. Makes about 5½ dozen bite-sized cookies.

Everything-But-The-Kitchen-Sink Cookies: Prepare as directed, substituting 2 cups total of any of the following for the nuts: raisins, toasted BAKER'S® ANGEL FLAKE® Coconut, dried cherries, chopped PLANTERS® Macadamias, dried cranberries, toasted PLANTERS® Slivered Almonds, dried chopped apricots, or dried mixed fruit bits.

Bar Cookies: Spread dough in greased, foil-lined 13×9-inch baking pan. Bake at 350°F for 22 to 24 minutes. Cool completely in pan on wire rack. Makes 2 dozen.

Make Ahead: After cookies are completely cooled, wrap in plastic wrap and place in an airtight plastic container or freezer zipper-style plastic bag. Freeze cookies up to 1 month. Bring cookies to room temperature before serving.

Freezing Cookie Dough: Freeze ¼ cupfuls of dough on cookie sheet 1 hour. Transfer to airtight plastic container or freezer zipper-style plastic bag. Freeze up to 1 month. Bake frozen dough on ungreased cookie sheet at 350°F for 20 to 23 minutes.

Chocolate Bliss Cookies

Chocolate Peanut Butter Cup Cookies

1 cup semisweet chocolate chips
2 squares (1 ounce each) unsweetened baking chocolate
1 cup sugar
½ Butter Flavor CRISCO® Stick or ½ cup Butter Flavor CRISCO®
    all-vegetable shortening
2 eggs
1 teaspoon salt
1 teaspoon vanilla
1½ cups plus 2 tablespoons all-purpose flour
½ teaspoon baking soda
¾ cup finely chopped peanuts
36 miniature peanut butter cups, unwrapped
1 cup peanut butter chips

1. Heat oven to 350°F. Place sheets of foil on countertop for cooling cookies.

2. Combine chocolate chips and chocolate squares in microwave-safe measuring cup or bowl. Microwave at 50% power (MEDIUM). Stir after 2 minutes. Repeat until smooth (or melt on rangetop in small saucepan over very low heat). Cool slightly.

3. Combine sugar and ½ cup shortening in large bowl. Beat at medium speed of electric mixer until blended and crumbly. Beat in eggs, one at a time, then salt and vanilla. Reduce speed to low. Add chocolate slowly. Mix until well blended. Stir in flour and baking soda with spoon until well blended. Shape dough into 1¼-inch balls. Roll in nuts. Place 2 inches apart on ungreased baking sheet.

4. Bake at 350°F for 8 to 10 minutes or until set. *Do not overbake.* Press peanut butter cup into center of each cookie immediately. Cool 2 minutes on baking sheet. Remove cookies to foil to cool completely.

5. Place peanut butter chips in heavy resealable sandwich bag. Seal. Microwave at 50% power (MEDIUM). Knead bag after 1 minute. Repeat until smooth (or melt by placing bag in hot water). Cut tiny tip off corner of bag. Squeeze out and drizzle over cookies.   *Makes 3 dozen cookies*

Chocolate Peanut Butter Cup Cookies

Super Chocolate Cookies

   2 cups all-purpose flour
   ⅓ cup unsweetened cocoa powder
   1 teaspoon baking soda
   ½ teaspoon salt
1⅓ cups packed brown sugar
   ½ cup (1 stick) butter, softened
   ½ cup shortening
   2 eggs
   2 teaspoons vanilla
   1 cup candy-coated chocolate pieces
   1 cup raisins
   ¾ cup salted peanuts, coarsely chopped

1. Preheat oven to 350°F. Combine flour, cocoa, baking soda and salt in medium bowl; set aside.

2. Beat brown sugar, butter and shortening in large bowl with electric mixer at medium speed until light and fluffy. Beat in eggs and vanilla until well blended. Gradually add flour mixture, beating at low speed until blended. Stir in candy pieces, raisins and peanuts.

3. Drop dough by ¼ cupfuls onto ungreased cookie sheets, spacing 3 inches apart. Flatten slightly with fingertips. Bake cookies 13 to 15 minutes or until almost set. Cool 2 minutes on cookie sheets. Transfer to wire racks. Cool completely.

Makes about 20 (4-inch) cookies

Super Chocolate Cookies

Toffee Chunk Brownie Cookies

    1 cup (2 sticks) butter
    4 ounces unsweetened chocolate, coarsely chopped
 1 ½ cups sugar
    2 eggs
    1 tablespoon vanilla
    3 cups all-purpose flour
    ⅛ teaspoon salt
 1 ½ cups coarsely chopped chocolate-covered toffee bars

Preheat oven to 350°F. Melt butter and chocolate in large saucepan over low heat, stirring until smooth. Remove from heat; cool slightly. Stir sugar into chocolate mixture until smooth. Stir in eggs until well blended. Stir in vanilla until smooth. Stir in flour and salt just until mixed. Fold in chopped toffee bars. Drop heaping tablespoonfuls of dough 1 ½ inches apart onto ungreased cookie sheets.

Bake 12 minutes or until just set. Let cookies stand on cookie sheets 5 minutes; transfer to wire racks to cool completely. Store in airtight container.

Makes 36 cookies

Double Chocolate Oat Cookies

    2 cups (12 ounces) semisweet chocolate pieces, divided
    ½ cup (1 stick) margarine or butter, softened
    ½ cup granulated sugar
    1 egg
    ¼ teaspoon vanilla
    ¾ cup all-purpose flour
    ¾ cup QUAKER® Oats (quick or old fashioned, uncooked)
    1 teaspoon baking powder
    ¼ teaspoon baking soda
    ¼ teaspoon salt (optional)

Preheat oven to 375°F. Melt 1 cup chocolate pieces in small saucepan; set aside. Beat margarine and sugar until fluffy; add melted chocolate, egg and vanilla. Add combined flour, oats, baking powder, baking soda and salt; mix well. Stir in remaining chocolate pieces. Drop by rounded tablespoonfuls onto *ungreased* cookie sheets. Bake 8 to 10 minutes. Cool 1 minute on cookie sheets; remove to wire racks.

Makes about 3 dozen cookies

Toffee Chunk Brownie Cookies

Design Your Own Chocolate Cookies

1 cup (2 sticks) butter, softened
1 cup granulated sugar
¾ cup packed light brown sugar
2 teaspoons vanilla extract
½ teaspoon salt
2 eggs
2 cups all-purpose flour
½ cup HERSHEY'S Cocoa
1 teaspoon baking soda

1. Heat oven to 375°F.

2. Beat butter, granulated sugar, brown sugar, vanilla and salt in large bowl until creamy. Add eggs; beat well.

3. Stir together flour, cocoa and baking soda; gradually add to butter mixture, beating until well blended. Drop by rounded teaspoons onto ungreased cookie sheet.

4. Bake 8 to 10 minutes or until set. Cool slightly; remove from cookie sheet to wire rack. Cool completely. *Makes about 5 dozen cookies*

Chocolate Chocolate Chip Cookies: Add 2 cups (one 12- or 11.5-ounce package) HERSHEY'S Semi-Sweet MINI CHIPS™, SPECIAL DARK® or Milk Chocolate Chips to basic chocolate batter.

Mini Kisses® Chocolate Cookies: Add 1¾ cups (10-ounce package) HERSHEY'S MINI KISSES® Milk or Semi-Sweet Chocolates to basic chocolate batter.

Mint Chocolate Chip Cookies: Add 1⅔ cups (10-ounce package) HERSHEY'S Mint Chocolate Chips to basic chocolate batter.

Chocolate Cookies with White Chips: Add 1⅔ cups (10-ounce package) HERSHEY'S Premier White Chips to basic chocolate batter.

Chocolate Cookies with Peanut Butter Chips: Add 1⅔ cups (one 10- or 11-ounce package) REESE'S® Peanut Butter Chips or REESE'S® Peanut Butter and Milk Chocolate Chips to basic chocolate batter.

Chocolate Cookies with Toffee: Add 1 to 1¼ cups HEATH® BITS 'O BRICKLE® Almond Toffee Bits, HEATH® Milk Chocolate Toffee Bits or SKOR® English Toffee Bits to basic chocolate batter. Lightly grease or paper-line cookie sheets.

Chocolate Cookies with White Chips, Chocolate Cookies with Peanut Butter Chips

Mocha Crinkles

1⅓ **cups packed light brown sugar**
 ½ **cup vegetable oil**
 ¼ **cup reduced-fat sour cream**
  1 **egg**
  1 **teaspoon vanilla**
1¾ **cups all-purpose flour**
 ¾ **cup unsweetened cocoa powder**
  2 **teaspoons instant espresso or coffee granules**
  1 **teaspoon baking soda**
 ¼ **teaspoon salt**
 ⅛ **teaspoon black pepper**
 ½ **cup powdered sugar**

1. Beat brown sugar and oil in medium bowl with electric mixer. Mix in sour cream, egg and vanilla. Set aside.

2. Mix flour, cocoa, espresso, baking soda, salt and pepper in another medium bowl.

3. Add flour mixture to brown sugar mixture; mix well. Refrigerate dough until firm, 3 to 4 hours.

4. Preheat oven to 350°F. Pour powdered sugar into shallow bowl. Roll dough into 1-inch balls. Roll balls in powdered sugar.

5. Bake on ungreased cookie sheets 10 to 12 minutes or until tops of cookies are firm to touch. (Do not overbake.) Cool on wire racks.

Makes about 6 dozen cookies

Mocha Crinkles

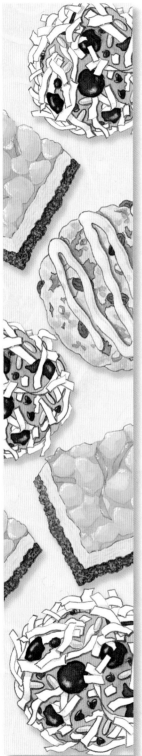

no-bake delights

Springtime Nests

    1 cup butterscotch chips
    ½ cup light corn syrup
    ½ cup creamy peanut butter
    ⅓ cup sugar
  2½ cups chow mein noodles
    2 cups cornflakes, slightly crushed
      Jelly beans or malted milk egg candies

1. Combine butterscotch chips, corn syrup, peanut butter and sugar in large microwavable bowl. Microwave at HIGH 1 to 1½ minutes or until melted and smooth, stirring at 30-second intervals.

2. Stir in chow mein noodles and cornflakes until evenly coated. Quickly shape scant ¼ cupfuls mixture into balls; make indentation in centers to make nests. Place nests on waxed paper to set. Place 3 jelly beans in each nest.   *Makes 1½ dozen cookies*

Peanut Butter Crispy Treats

    4 cups toasted rice cereal
  1¾ cups "M&M's"® Milk Chocolate Mini Baking Bits
    4 cups mini marshmallows
    ½ cup creamy peanut butter
    ¼ cup butter or margarine
    ¼ teaspoon salt

Combine cereal and "M&M's"® Milk Chocolate Mini Baking Bits in lightly greased baking pan. Melt marshmallows, peanut butter, butter and salt in heavy saucepan over low heat, stirring occasionally, until mixture is smooth. Pour melted mixture over cereal mixture, tossing lightly until thoroughly coated. Gently shape into 1½-inch balls with buttered fingers. Place on waxed paper; cool at room temperature until set. Store in tightly covered container.   *Makes about 3 dozen*

Springtime Nests

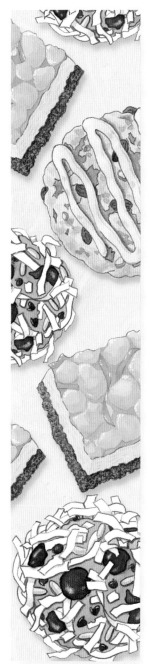

No-Bake Chocolate Peanut Butter Bars

2 cups peanut butter, *divided*
¾ cup (1½ sticks) butter, softened
2 cups powdered sugar, *divided*
3 cups graham cracker crumbs
2 cups (12-ounce package) NESTLÉ® TOLL HOUSE®
 Semi-Sweet Chocolate Mini Morsels, *divided*

GREASE 13×9-inch baking pan.

BEAT *1¼ cups* peanut butter and butter in large mixer bowl until creamy. Gradually beat in *1 cup* powdered sugar. With hands or wooden spoon, work in *remaining* powdered sugar, graham cracker crumbs and *½ cup* morsels. Press evenly into prepared pan. Smooth top with spatula.

MELT *remaining* peanut butter and *remaining* morsels in medium, *heavy-duty* saucepan over *lowest possible heat,* stirring constantly, until smooth. Spread over graham cracker crust in pan. Refrigerate for at least 1 hour or until chocolate is firm; cut into bars. Store in refrigerator. *Makes 5 dozen bars*

Citrus Cream Bars

1¼ cups finely crushed chocolate sandwich cookies
⅔ cup butter, softened, divided
1½ cups powdered sugar
 1 tablespoon milk
1½ teaspoons grated orange peel
 ½ teaspoon lemon peel
 ½ teaspoon vanilla
 ¼ cup semisweet chocolate chips, melted

1. Combine cookie crumbs and ⅓ cup butter in medium bowl. Press onto bottom of ungreased 9-inch square baking pan. Refrigerate until firm.

2. Combine powdered sugar, remaining ⅓ cup butter, milk, orange peel, lemon peel and vanilla in small bowl. Beat with electric mixer at medium speed, scraping bowl often, until light and fluffy. Spread over crust.

3. Drizzle melted chocolate over filling. Refrigerate until firm, about 2 hours. Cut into bars. Store leftovers in refrigerator. *Makes about 2 dozen bars*

No-Bake Chocolate Peanut Butter Bars

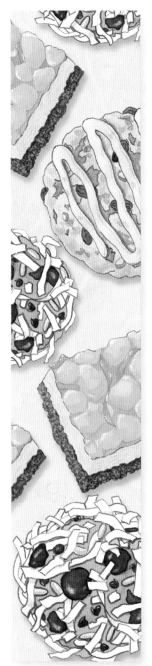

No-Bake Cherry Crisps

   1 cup powdered sugar
   1 cup peanut butter
   ¼ cup (½ stick) butter, softened
 1⅓ cups crisp rice cereal
   ½ cup maraschino cherries, drained, dried and chopped
   ¼ cup plus 2 tablespoons mini semisweet chocolate chips
   ¼ cup chopped pecans
   1 to 2 cups flaked coconut

Beat powdered sugar, peanut butter and butter in large bowl. Stir in cereal, cherries, chocolate chips and pecans. Mix well. Shape teaspoonfuls of dough into 1-inch balls. Roll in coconut. Place on cookie sheets and refrigerate 1 hour. Store in refrigerator.

Makes about 3 dozen cookies

Fudgey Cocoa No-Bake Treats

   2 cups sugar
   ½ cup (1 stick) butter or margarine
   ½ cup milk
   ⅓ cup HERSHEY¿S Cocoa
   ⅔ cup REESE'S® Crunchy Peanut Butter
   3 cups quick-cooking rolled oats
   ½ cup chopped peanuts (optional)
   2 teaspoons vanilla extract

1. Place piece of wax paper or foil on tray or cookie sheet. Combine sugar, butter, milk and cocoa in medium saucepan.

2. Cook over medium heat, stirring constantly, until mixture comes to a rolling boil.

3. Remove from heat; cool 1 minute.

4. Add peanut butter, oats, peanuts, if desired, and vanilla; stir to mix well. Quickly drop mixture by heaping teaspoons onto wax paper or foil. Cool completely. Store in cool, dry place.

Makes about 4 dozen

Prep Time: 20 minutes
Cook Time: 5 minutes
Cool Time: 30 minutes

No-Bake Cherry Crisps

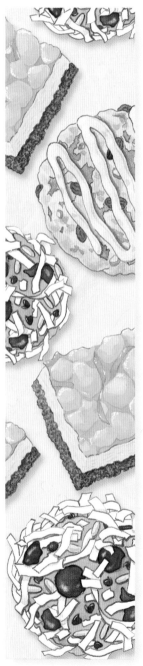

No-Bake Pineapple Marmalade Squares

1 cup graham cracker crumbs
½ cup plus 2 tablespoons sugar, divided
¼ cup light margarine, melted
1 cup fat free or light sour cream
4 ounces light cream cheese, softened
¼ cup orange marmalade or apricot fruit spread, divided
1 can (20 ounces) DOLE® Crushed Pineapple
1 envelope unflavored gelatin

• Combine graham cracker crumbs, 2 tablespoons sugar and margarine in 8-inch square glass baking dish; pat mixture firmly and evenly onto bottom of dish. Freeze 10 minutes.

• Beat sour cream, cream cheese, remaining ½ cup sugar and 1 tablespoon marmalade in medium bowl until smooth and blended; set aside.

• Drain crushed pineapple, reserving ¼ cup juice.

• Sprinkle gelatin over reserved juice in small saucepan; let stand 1 minute. Cook and stir over low heat until gelatin dissolves.

• Beat gelatin mixture into sour cream mixture until well blended. Spoon mixture evenly over crust.

• Stir together crushed pineapple and remaining 3 tablespoons marmalade in small bowl until blended. Evenly spoon over sour cream filling. Cover and refrigerate 2 hours or until firm. *Makes 16 servings*

No-Bake Pineapple Marmalade Squares

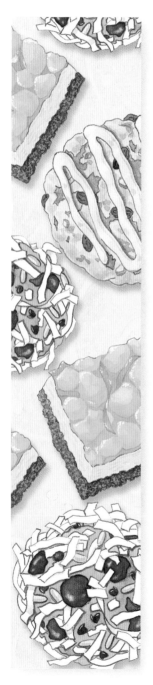

Scotcheroos

Nonstick cooking spray
1½ **cups creamy peanut butter**
1 **cup granulated sugar**
1 **cup light corn syrup**
6 **cups toasted rice cereal**
1⅔ **cups (11-ounce package) NESTLÉ® TOLL HOUSE®**
Butterscotch Flavored Morsels
1 **cup (6 ounces) NESTLÉ® TOLL HOUSE®**
Semi-Sweet Chocolate Morsels

COAT 13×9-inch baking pan with cooking spray.

COMBINE peanut butter, sugar and corn syrup in large saucepan. Cook over medium-low heat, stirring frequently, until melted. Remove from heat. Add cereal; stir until thoroughly coated. Press onto bottom of prepared baking pan.

MICROWAVE butterscotch morsels and semi-sweet chocolate morsels in large, uncovered, microwave-safe bowl on HIGH (100%) power for 1 minute. STIR. Morsels may retain some of their original shape. If necessary, microwave at additional 10- to 15-second intervals, stirring just until morsels are melted. Spread over cereal mixture.

REFRIGERATE for 15 to 20 minutes or until topping is firm. Cut into bars.

Makes 2½ dozen bars

P.B. Graham Snackers

½ **Butter Flavor CRISCO® Stick or ½ cup Butter Flavor CRISCO®
   all-vegetable shortening**
2 **cups confectioners' sugar**
¾ **cup JIF® Creamy Peanut Butter**
1 **cup graham cracker crumbs**
½ **cup semisweet chocolate chips**
½ **cup graham cracker crumbs, crushed peanuts, colored sugar or
   sprinkles (optional)**

1. Combine ½ cup shortening, confectioners' sugar and peanut butter in large bowl. Beat at low speed of electric mixer until well blended. Stir in 1 cup crumbs and chocolate chips. Cover and refrigerate 1 hour.

2. Form dough into 1-inch balls. Roll in ½ cup crumbs, peanuts, colored sugar or sprinkles. Cover and refrigerate until ready to serve.   *Makes about 3 dozen cookies*

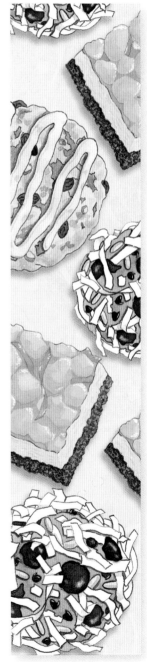

Monkey Bars

3 **cups miniature marshmallows**
½ **cup honey**
⅓ **cup butter**
¼ **cup peanut butter**
2 **teaspoons vanilla**
¼ **teaspoon salt**
4 **cups crispy rice cereal**
2 **cups rolled oats, uncooked**
½ **cup flaked coconut**
¼ **cup peanuts**

Combine marshmallows, honey, butter, peanut butter, vanilla and salt in medium saucepan. Melt marshmallow mixture over low heat, stirring constantly. Combine rice cereal, oats, coconut and peanuts in 13×9×2-inch baking pan. Pour marshmallow mixture over dry ingredients. Mix until thoroughly coated. Press mixture firmly into pan. Cool completely before cutting.   *Makes 2 dozen bars*

Microwave Directions: Microwave marshmallows, honey, butter, peanut butter, vanilla and salt in 2-quart microwave-safe bowl on HIGH 2½ to 3 minutes. Continue as above.

Favorite recipe from **National Honey Board**

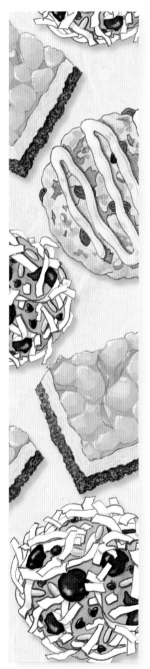

No-Bake Chocolate Oat Bars

> 1 cup (2 sticks) butter
> ½ cup packed brown sugar
> 1 teaspoon vanilla
> 3 cups uncooked quick oats
> 1 cup semisweet chocolate chips
> ½ cup crunchy or creamy peanut butter

Grease 9-inch square baking pan. Melt butter in large saucepan over medium heat. Add brown sugar and vanilla; mix well. Stir in oats. Cook over low heat 2 to 3 minutes or until ingredients are well blended. Press half of mixture into prepared pan. Use back of large spoon to spread mixture evenly.

Meanwhile, melt chocolate chips in small heavy saucepan over low heat, stirring occasionally. Stir in peanut butter. Pour chocolate mixture over oat mixture in pan; spread evenly with knife or back of spoon. Crumble remaining oat mixture over chocolate layer, pressing down gently. Cover and refrigerate 2 to 3 hours or overnight. Bring to room temperature before cutting into bars. (Bars can be frozen; let thaw at least 10 minutes before serving.)   *Makes 32 bars*

3-Minute No-Bake Cookies

> 2 cups granulated sugar
> ½ cup (1 stick) margarine or butter
> ½ cup 2% milk
> ⅓ cup unsweetened cocoa powder
> 3 cups QUAKER® Oats (quick or old fashioned, uncooked)

In large saucepan, combine sugar, margarine, milk and cocoa. Bring to a boil over medium heat, stirring frequently. Continue boiling 3 minutes. Remove from heat. Stir in oats; mix well. Quickly drop by tablespoonfuls onto waxed paper or greased cookie sheet. Let stand until set. Store tightly covered at room temperature.

Makes about 3 dozen cookies

No-Bake Chocolate Oat Bars

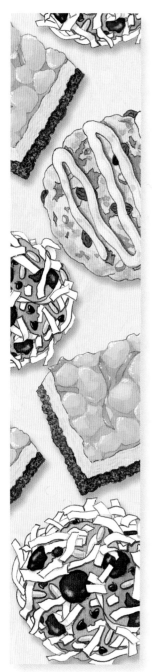

Special Treat No-Bake Squares

Crust
   ½ cup (1 stick) butter
   ¼ cup granulated sugar
   ¼ cup unsweetened cocoa powder
    1 egg
   ¼ teaspoon salt
 1½ cups graham cracker crumbs
   ¾ cup flaked coconut
   ½ cup chopped pecans

Filling
   ⅓ cup butter, softened
    1 package (3 ounces) cream cheese, softened
    1 teaspoon vanilla
    1 cup powdered sugar

Glaze
    1 (2-ounce) dark sweet or bittersweet candy bar, broken into
       ½-inch pieces
    1 teaspoon butter

Line 9-inch square baking pan with foil, shiny side up, allowing 2-inch overhang on sides. Set aside.

For crust, combine ½ cup butter, granulated sugar, cocoa, egg and salt in medium saucepan. Cook over medium heat, stirring constantly, until mixture thickens, about 2 minutes. Remove from heat; stir in graham cracker crumbs, coconut and pecans. Press evenly into prepared baking pan.

For filling, beat ⅓ cup softened butter, cream cheese and vanilla in small bowl until smooth. Gradually beat in powdered sugar. Spread over crust; refrigerate 30 minutes.

For glaze, combine candy bar pieces and 1 teaspoon butter in small resealable plastic food storage bag; seal bag. Microwave at HIGH 50 seconds. Turn bag over; microwave 40 to 50 seconds or until melted. Knead bag until chocolate is smooth. Cut tiny corner off bag; drizzle chocolate over filling. Refrigerate until firm, about 20 minutes. Remove bars from pan using foil. Cut into 1½-inch squares.

Makes about 3 dozen squares

Special Treat No-Bake Squares

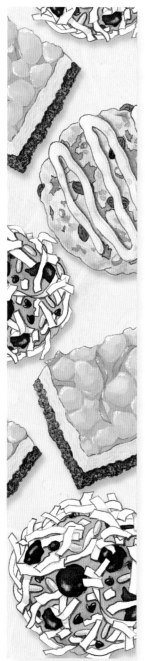

No-Bake Gingersnap Balls

20 gingersnap cookies (about 5 ounces)
3 tablespoons dark corn syrup
2 tablespoons creamy peanut butter
⅓ cup powdered sugar

1. Place cookies in large resealable plastic food storage bag; crush finely with rolling pin or meat mallet.

2. Combine corn syrup and peanut butter in medium bowl. Add crushed gingersnaps; mix well. (Mixture should hold together without being sticky. If mixture is too dry, stir in additional 1 or 2 tablespoons corn syrup.)

3. Shape mixture into 24 (1-inch) balls; roll in powdered sugar.

Makes 2 dozen cookies

Note: Some gingersnaps are crisper than others, so you might need to add an extra 1 or 2 tablespoons of corn syrup to the crumb mixture in order to hold it together.

No-Bake Banana Peanut Butter Fudge Bars

1 ripe, large DOLE® Banana
⅔ cup butter or margarine
2 teaspoons vanilla extract
2½ cups rolled oats
½ cup packed brown sugar
1 cup semisweet chocolate chips
½ cup peanut butter

● Finely chop banana to measure 1¼ cups. Melt butter in large skillet over medium heat; stir in vanilla. Add oats and brown sugar. Heat and stir 5 minutes. Set aside ¾ cup oat mixture. Press remaining oat mixture into greased 9-inch square baking pan. Sprinkle banana over crust.

● Melt chocolate chips and peanut butter together over low heat. Pour and spread over banana. Sprinkle with reserved oat mixture; press down lightly. Chill 2 hours before cutting. Store in refrigerator.

Makes 24 bars

No-Bake Gingersnap Balls

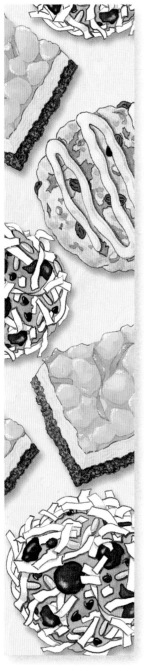

No-Bake Butterscotch Haystacks

1 cup HERSHEY'S Butterscotch Chips
½ cup REESE'S® Peanut Butter Chips
1 tablespoon shortening (do not use butter, margarine, spread
or oil)
1½ cups (3-ounce can) chow mein noodles, coarsely broken

1. Line cookie sheet with wax paper. Place butterscotch chips, peanut butter chips and shortening in medium microwave-safe bowl.

2. Microwave at HIGH (100%) 1 minute; stir. If necessary, microwave at HIGH an additional 15 seconds at a time, stirring after each heating, just until chips are melted and mixture is smooth when stirred.

3. Immediately add chow mein noodles; stir to coat. Drop mixture by heaping teaspoons onto prepared cookie sheet or into paper candy cups; let stand until firm. If necessary, cover and refrigerate until firm. Store in refrigerator in tightly covered container.   *Makes about 2 dozen cookies*

Chocolate Haystacks: Substitute 1 cup HERSHEY'S Semi-Sweet Chocolate Chips or HERSHEY'S Milk Chocolate Chips for butterscotch chips. Proceed as directed above with peanut butter chips, shortening and chow mein noodles.

Prep Time: 15 minutes
Cook Time: 1 minute
Cool Time: 30 minutes

Conversation Heart Cereal Treats

20 large marshmallows
2 tablespoons butter or margarine
3 cups frosted oat cereal with marshmallow bits
12 large conversation hearts

1. Line 8- or 9-inch square pan with aluminum foil, leaving 2-inch overhangs on 2 sides. Generously grease or spray with nonstick cooking spray.

2. Melt marshmallows and butter in medium saucepan over medium heat 3 minutes or until melted and smooth, stirring constantly. Remove from heat.

3. Add cereal; stir until completely coated. Spread in prepared pan; press evenly onto bottom using greased rubber spatula. Press heart candies into top of treats while still warm, evenly spacing to allow 1 heart per bar. Let cool 10 minutes. Using foil overhangs as handles, remove treats from pan. Cut into bars. *Makes 12 bars*

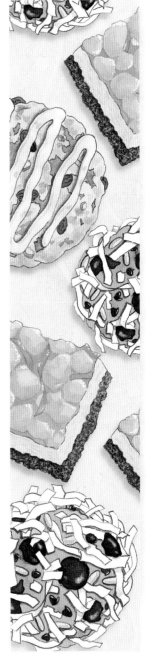

Chewy Chocolate No-Bakes

1 cup (6 ounces) semisweet chocolate pieces
16 large marshmallows
⅓ cup (5 tablespoons plus 1 teaspoon) margarine or butter
2 cups QUAKER® Oats (quick or old fashioned, uncooked)
1 cup (any combination of) raisins, diced dried mixed fruit, flaked coconut, miniature marshmallows or chopped nuts
1 teaspoon vanilla

In large saucepan over low heat, melt chocolate pieces, marshmallows and margarine, stirring until smooth. Remove from heat; cool slightly. Stir in remaining ingredients. Drop by rounded teaspoonfuls onto waxed paper. Chill 2 to 3 hours. Let stand at room temperature about 15 minutes before serving. Store in tightly covered container in refrigerator. *Makes 3 dozen cookies*

Microwave Directions: Place chocolate pieces, margarine and marshmallows in large microwavable bowl. Microwave on HIGH 1 to 2 minutes or until mixture is melted and smooth, stirring every 30 seconds. Proceed as recipe directs.

cookies for kids

Lollipop Sugar Cookies

1¼ cups granulated sugar
  1 Butter Flavor CRISCO® Stick or 1 cup Butter Flavor CRISCO®
    all-vegetable shortening
  2 eggs
¼ cup light corn syrup or regular pancake syrup
  1 tablespoon vanilla
  3 cups all-purpose flour
¾ teaspoon baking powder
½ teaspoon baking soda
½ teaspoon salt
36 flat ice cream sticks
    Any of the following decorations: miniature baking chips, raisins,
    red hots, nonpareils, colored sugar or nuts

1. Combine sugar and 1 cup shortening in large bowl. Beat at medium speed of electric mixer until well blended. Add eggs, syrup and vanilla; beat until well blended and fluffy.

2. Combine flour, baking powder, baking soda and salt. Add gradually to creamed mixture at low speed until well blended. Wrap dough in plastic wrap. Refrigerate at least 1 hour.

3. Heat oven to 375°F. Place foil on countertop for cooling cookies.

4. Shape dough into 1½-inch balls. Push ice cream stick into center of each ball. Place balls 3 inches apart on ungreased baking sheet. Flatten balls to ½-inch thickness with bottom of greased and floured glass. Decorate as desired; press decorations gently into dough.*

5. Bake at 375°F for 8 to 10 minutes. *Do not overbake.* Cool on baking sheet 2 minutes. Remove cookies to foil to cool completely.

Makes about 3 dozen cookies

Cookies can also be painted before baking. Mix 1 egg yolk and ¼ teaspoon water. Divide into 3 small cups. Add 2 to 3 drops food color to each. Stir. Use clean water color brushes to paint designs on cookies.

Lollipop Sugar Cookies

Worm Cookies

1¾ cups all-purpose flour
¾ cup powdered sugar
¼ cup unsweetened cocoa powder
⅛ teaspoon salt
1 cup (2 sticks) butter
1 teaspoon vanilla
1 tube white frosting

1. Combine flour, sugar, cocoa and salt; set aside. Combine butter and vanilla in large bowl. Beat with electric mixer at medium-low speed until fluffy. Gradually beat in flour mixture until well combined. Cover and chill dough at least 30 minutes before rolling.

2. Preheat oven to 350°F. Form dough into 1½-inch balls. Roll balls gently to form 5- to 6-inch logs about ½ inch thick. Shape into worms 2 inches apart on ungreased cookie sheets.

3. Bake 12 minutes or until set. Let stand on cookie sheets until cooled completely. Pipe eyes and stripes with white frosting. *Makes about 3 dozen cookies*

Peanut Butter and Jelly Thumbprints

1½ cups all-purpose flour
½ cup sugar
½ teaspoon baking soda
¼ teaspoon salt
¾ cup PETER PAN® Creamy Peanut Butter
¼ cup butter, softened
¼ cup honey
1 tablespoon milk
KNOTT'S BERRY FARM® Grape Jelly or any favorite flavor

In large bowl, combine flour, sugar, baking soda and salt. Add peanut butter and butter; mix until crumbly. Stir in honey and milk. Shape into 1-inch balls. Place 2 inches apart on ungreased baking sheets. Press thumb into center of each ball; place ½ *teaspoon* jelly in each thumbprint. Bake at 375°F for 8 to 10 minutes. Cool on baking sheets 1 minute before removing to wire racks. Store in airtight container.

Makes 2 dozen cookies

Worm Cookies

Giant Peanut Butter Cup Cookies

½ cup (1 stick) butter or margarine, softened
¾ cup sugar
⅓ cup REESE'S® Creamy or Crunchy Peanut Butter
1 egg
½ teaspoon vanilla extract
1¼ cups all-purpose flour
½ teaspoon baking soda
¼ teaspoon salt
16 REESE'S® Peanut Butter Cups Miniatures, cut into fourths

1. Heat oven to 350°F.

2. Beat butter, sugar and peanut butter in medium bowl until creamy. Add egg and vanilla; beat well. Stir together flour, baking soda and salt. Add to butter mixture; blend well. Drop dough by level ¼ cup measurements onto ungreased cookie sheets, three cookies per sheet. (Cookies will spread while baking.) Push about seven pieces of peanut butter cup into each cookie, flattening cookie slightly.

3. Bake 15 to 17 minutes or until light golden brown around edges. Centers will be pale and slightly soft. Cool 1 minute on cookie sheet. Remove to wire rack; cool completely. *Makes 9 cookies*

Giant Peanut Butter Cup Cookies

Dandy Candy Oatmeal Cookies

1 jar (12 ounces) JIF® Creamy Peanut Butter
1 cup granulated sugar
1 cup firmly packed brown sugar
½ Butter Flavor CRISCO® Stick or ½ cup Butter Flavor CRISCO®
    all-vegetable shortening plus additional for greasing
 3 eggs
¾ teaspoon vanilla
¾ teaspoon maple (or maple-blend) syrup
4½ cups quick oats (not instant or old-fashioned), uncooked, divided
  2 teaspoons baking soda
  1 package (8 ounces) candy-coated chocolate pieces

1. Heat oven to 350°F. Grease baking sheet with shortening. Place sheets of foil on countertop for cooling cookies.

2. Combine peanut butter, granulated sugar, brown sugar and ½ cup shortening in large bowl. Beat at medium speed of electric mixer until well blended and fluffy. Add eggs, vanilla and maple syrup. Beat at high speed 3 to 4 minutes. Add 2¼ cups oats and baking soda; stir. Stir in candy. Stir in remaining 2¼ cups oats. Shape dough into 1½-inch balls. Flatten slightly. Place 2 inches apart on prepared baking sheet.

3. Bake for 9 to 10 minutes for chewy cookies or 11 to 12 minutes for crispy cookies. Cool 2 minutes. Remove cookies to foil to cool completely.

Makes 3½ dozen cookies

Dandy Candy Oatmeal Cookies

Peanut Butter Bears

2 cups uncooked quick oats
2 cups all-purpose flour
1 tablespoon baking powder
1 cup granulated sugar
¾ cup (1½ sticks) butter, softened
½ cup packed brown sugar
½ cup creamy peanut butter
2 eggs
1 teaspoon vanilla
3 tablespoons miniature chocolate chips

1. Combine oats, flour and baking powder in medium bowl; set aside.

2. Beat granulated sugar, butter, brown sugar and peanut butter in large bowl with electric mixer at medium-high speed until creamy. Add eggs and vanilla; beat until light and fluffy. Add oat mixture. Beat on low speed until combined. Cover and refrigerate 1 to 2 hours or until easy to handle.

3. Preheat oven to 375°F.

4. For each bear, shape one 1-inch ball for body and one ¾-inch ball for head. Place body and head together on cookie sheet; flatten slightly. Shape 7 small balls for ears, arms, legs and mouth; arrange on bear body and head. Place 2 chocolate chips on each head for eyes; place 1 chocolate chip on each body for belly-button.

5. Bake 9 to 11 minutes or until light brown. Cool 1 minute on cookie sheets. Remove to wire racks; cool completely.   *Makes 4 dozen cookies*

Peanut Butter Bear

Lady Bugs

¾ cup shortening
½ cup sugar
¼ cup honey
1 egg
½ teaspoon vanilla
2 cups all-purpose flour
⅓ cup cornmeal
1 teaspoon baking powder
½ teaspoon salt
  Orange and black icings and yellow candy-coated chocolate pieces

1. Beat shortening, sugar and honey in large bowl with electric mixer at medium speed until light and fluffy. Add egg and vanilla; mix until well blended. Combine flour, cornmeal, baking powder and salt in medium bowl. Add to shortening mixture; mix at low speed until blended. Shape dough into disc. Wrap in plastic wrap and chill 2 hours or overnight.

2. Preheat oven to 375°F. Divide dough into 24 equal sections. Shape each section into 2×1¼-inch oval. Place ovals 2 inches apart on ungreased cookie sheets.

3. Bake 10 to 12 minutes or until lightly browned. Cool on cookie sheets 2 minutes. Remove to wire racks; cool completely.

4. Decorate cookies with orange and black icings and candy-coated pieces to resemble lady bugs.   *Makes 2 dozen cookies*

Lady Bugs

Chocolate Marshmallow Thumbprints

¾ cup (1½ sticks) butter, softened
½ cup granulated sugar
1 large egg
1 teaspoon vanilla extract
1½ cups all-purpose flour
2 tablespoons unsweetened cocoa powder
¼ teaspoon salt
1¼ cups "M&M's"® Chocolate Mini Baking Bits, divided
¼ cup marshmallow cream
¼ cup vanilla frosting

Preheat oven to 350°F. Lightly grease cookie sheets; set aside. In large bowl cream butter and sugar until light and fluffy; beat in egg and vanilla. In medium bowl combine flour, cocoa powder and salt; add to creamed mixture. Stir in 1 cup "M&M's"® Chocolate Mini Baking Bits. Roll dough into 1-inch balls and place about 2 inches apart on prepared cookie sheets. Make indentation in center of each ball with thumb. Bake 10 minutes. Remove from oven and re-indent; bake 1 minute. Cool completely on wire racks. In small bowl combine marshmallow cream and frosting. Fill each indentation with about ½ teaspoon marshmallow mixture. Sprinkle with remaining ¼ cup "M&M's"® Chocolate Mini Baking Bits. Store between layers of waxed paper in tightly covered container.   *Makes 3 dozen cookies*

Banana Split Sundae Cookies

1 cup (2 sticks) margarine or butter, softened
1 cup firmly packed brown sugar
1½ cups mashed ripe bananas (about 4 medium)
2 eggs
2 teaspoons vanilla
2½ cups QUAKER® Oats (quick or old fashioned, uncooked)
2 cups all-purpose flour
1 teaspoon baking soda
¼ teaspoon salt (optional)
1 cup (6 ounces) semisweet chocolate pieces
Ice cream or frozen yogurt
Ice cream topping, any flavor

Heat oven to 350°F. Beat together margarine and sugar until creamy. Add bananas, eggs and vanilla; beat well. Add combined oats, flour, baking soda and salt; mix well. Stir in chocolate pieces; mix well. Drop by ¼ cupfuls onto ungreased cookie sheets about 3 inches apart. Spread dough to 3½-inch diameter. Bake 14 to 16 minutes or until edges are light golden brown. Cool 1 minute on cookie sheets; remove to wire racks. Cool completely. To serve, top each cookie with scoop of ice cream and ice cream topping. *Makes about 2 dozen cookies*

Happy Face Oatmeal Monsters

1½ cups all-purpose flour
1 teaspoon baking soda
½ teaspoon salt
1 cup (2 sticks) butter, softened
1 cup firmly packed light brown sugar
2 eggs
1 teaspoon vanilla
2 cups uncooked quick oats
Granulated sugar
28 candy-coated chocolate pieces or large chocolate chips
Cinnamon red hot candies or red licorice strings
Colored frosting in tube and flaked coconut (optional)

1. Preheat oven to 350°F.

2. Combine flour, baking soda and salt in small bowl; set aside. Beat butter and brown sugar in large bowl with electric mixer at medium speed until light and fluffy. Beat in eggs, 1 at a time, until well blended. Beat in vanilla. Gradually beat in flour mixture at low speed until blended. Stir in oats.

3. Drop dough by level ¼ cupfuls 3 inches apart onto ungreased cookie sheets. Flatten dough with bottom of glass that has been dipped in granulated sugar until dough is 2 inches in diameter. Press chocolate pieces into cookies for eyes; use cinnamon candies for mouth.

4. Bake 12 to 14 minutes or until cookies are set and edges are golden brown. Cool cookies 2 minutes on cookie sheets. Remove to wire racks; cool completely.

5. Decorate cookies with frosting and coconut for hair, if desired.
Makes about 14 (4-inch) cookies

Crayon Cookies

1 cup (2 sticks) butter, softened
2 teaspoons vanilla
½ cup powdered sugar
2¼ cups all-purpose flour
¼ teaspoon salt
Assorted paste food colorings
1½ cups chocolate chips
1½ teaspoons shortening

1. Preheat oven to 350°F. Grease cookie sheets.

2. Beat butter and vanilla in large bowl with electric mixer at high speed until fluffy. Add powdered sugar; beat at medium speed until blended. Combine flour and salt in small bowl. Gradually add to butter mixture.

3. Divide dough into 10 equal sections. Reserve 1 section; cover and refrigerate remaining 9 sections. Combine reserved section and desired food coloring in small bowl; blend well.

4. Cut dough in half. Roll each half into 5-inch log. Pinch one end to resemble crayon tip. Place cookies 2 inches apart on prepared cookie sheets. Repeat with remaining 9 sections of dough and desired food colorings.

5. Bake 15 to 18 minutes or until edges are lightly browned. Cool completely on cookie sheets.

6. Combine chocolate chips and shortening in small microwavable bowl. Microwave at HIGH 1 to 1½ minutes, stirring after 1 minute, or until chocolate is melted and smooth. Decorate cookies with chocolate mixture to look like crayons.

Makes 20 cookies

Crayon Cookies

Peanut Butter Pizza Cookies

1 ¼ cups firmly packed light brown sugar
¾ cup JIF® Creamy Peanut Butter
½ CRISCO® Stick or ½ cup CRISCO® all-vegetable shortening
3 tablespoons milk
1 tablespoon vanilla
1 egg
1 ¾ cups all-purpose flour
¾ teaspoon salt
¾ teaspoon baking soda
8 ounces white baking chocolate, chopped
Decorative candies

1. Heat oven to 375°F. Place sheets of foil on countertop for cooling cookies.

2. Combine brown sugar, peanut butter, ½ cup shortening, milk and vanilla in large bowl. Beat at medium speed of electric mixer until well blended. Add egg. Beat just until blended.

3. Combine flour, salt and baking soda. Add to creamed mixture at low speed. Mix just until blended.

4. Divide dough in half. Form each half into a ball. Place 1 ball of dough onto center of ungreased pizza pan or baking sheet. Spread dough with fingers to form 12-inch circle. Repeat with remaining ball of dough.

5. Bake one baking sheet at a time at 375°F for 10 to 12 minutes, or until lightly browned. *Do not overbake.* Cool 2 minutes on baking sheet. Remove with large spatula to foil to cool completely.

6. Place white chocolate in shallow microwave-safe bowl. Microwave at HIGH (100%) for 30 seconds. Stir. Repeat at 30-second intervals until white chocolate is melted.

7. Spread melted white chocolate on center of cooled cookies to within ½ inch of edge. Decorate with candies. Let set completely. Cut into wedges.

Makes 2 pizzas

Peanut Butter Pizza Cookie

Dino-Mite Dinosaurs

1 cup (2 sticks) butter, softened
1¼ cups granulated sugar
1 large egg
2 squares (1 ounce each) semi-sweet chocolate, melted
½ teaspoon vanilla extract
2⅓ cups all-purpose flour
1 teaspoon baking powder
¼ teaspoon salt
1 cup white frosting
   Assorted food colorings
1 cup "M&M's"® Chocolate Mini Baking Bits

In large bowl cream butter and sugar until light and fluffy; beat in egg, chocolate and vanilla. In medium bowl combine flour, baking powder and salt; add to creamed mixture. Wrap and refrigerate dough 2 to 3 hours. Preheat oven to 350°F. Working with half the dough at a time on lightly floured surface, roll to ¼-inch thickness. Cut into dinosaur shapes using 4-inch cookie cutters. Place about 2 inches apart on ungreased cookie sheets. Bake 10 to 12 minutes. Cool 2 minutes on cookie sheets; cool completely on wire racks. Tint frosting desired colors. Frost cookies and decorate with "M&M's"® Chocolate Mini Baking Bits. Store in tightly covered container.

Makes 2 dozen cookies

Dino-Mite Dinosaurs

Peanut Butter and Jelly Pinwheels

1 Butter Flavor CRISCO® Stick or 1 cup Butter Flavor CRISCO®
    All-Vegetable Shortening
1 cup JIF® Creamy Peanut Butter
¾ cup granulated sugar
¾ cup firmly packed light brown sugar
2 eggs
1 teaspoon vanilla
2½ cups all-purpose flour
1 teaspoon salt
1 teaspoon baking soda
½ cup SMUCKER'S® Seedless Red Raspberry Jam*
⅔ cup very finely chopped peanuts

*If desired, top with additional jam before serving.

Combine 1 cup shortening, peanut butter, granulated sugar and brown sugar in large bowl. Beat at medium speed of electric mixer until well blended. Beat in eggs and vanilla.

Combine flour, salt and baking soda. Add gradually to creamed mixture at low speed. Beat until well blended.

Cut parchment paper to line 17×11-inch pan. Press dough out to edges of paper. Spread with jam to within ½ inch of edges.

Lift up long side of paper. Loosen dough with spatula. Roll up dough jelly-roll fashion; seal seam. Sprinkle nuts on paper; roll dough over nuts. Press any remaining nuts into dough. Wrap rolled-up dough in parchment paper; place in plastic bag. Refrigerate overnight.

Preheat oven to 375°F.

Line baking sheet with foil or parchment paper. Unwrap dough and cut into ½-inch slices. Place 2 inches apart on prepared baking sheet.

Bake for 10 to 12 minutes or until set. Cool about 5 minutes on baking sheet before removing to new foil to cool completely.   *Makes 3 dozen cookies*

Peanut Butter and Jelly Pinwheels

Monster Pops

1⅔ cups all-purpose flour
1 teaspoon baking soda
½ teaspoon salt
1 cup (2 sticks) butter or margarine, softened
¾ cup granulated sugar
¾ cup packed brown sugar
2 teaspoons vanilla extract
2 large eggs
2 cups (12-ounce package) NESTLÉ® TOLL HOUSE®
Semi-Sweet Chocolate Morsels
2 cups quick or old-fashioned oats
1 cup raisins
About 24 wooden craft sticks
1 container (16 ounces) prepared vanilla frosting, colored as
desired, or colored icing in tubes
Colored candies (such as WONKA® RUNTS and/or NERDS)

PREHEAT oven to 325°F.

COMBINE flour, baking soda and salt in small bowl. Beat butter, granulated sugar, brown sugar and vanilla extract in large mixer bowl until creamy. Beat in eggs. Gradually beat in flour mixture. Stir in morsels, oats and raisins. Drop dough by level ¼-cup measure 3 inches apart onto ungreased baking sheets. Shape into round mounds. Insert wooden stick into side of each mound.

BAKE for 14 to 18 minutes or until golden brown. Cool on baking sheets on wire racks for 2 minutes; remove to wire racks to cool completely.

DECORATE pops as desired.   *Makes about 2 dozen cookies*

For Speedy Monster Pops: SUBSTITUTE 2 packages (18 ounces each), NESTLÉ® TOLL HOUSE® Refrigerated Chocolate Chip Cookie Dough for the nine ingredients, adding 1 cup quick or old-fashioned oats and ½ cup raisins to the dough. Bake as stated above for 16 to 20 minutes or until golden brown. Makes 1½ dozen cookies.

Monster Pops

holiday
treats

Swedish Spritz

**1 Butter Flavor CRISCO® Stick or 1 cup Butter Flavor CRISCO®
    all-vegetable shortening**
1 cup granulated sugar
1 egg
1 tablespoon milk
1 teaspoon almond extract
2 cups all-purpose flour
½ cup finely ground blanched almonds
¼ teaspoon salt
⅛ teaspoon baking powder
    Colored sugar crystals (optional)

1. Heat oven to 350°F. Refrigerate ungreased baking sheet. Place sheets of foil on countertop for cooling cookies.

2. Combine 1 cup shortening and granulated sugar in large bowl. Beat at medium speed of electric mixer until well blended. Beat in egg, milk and almond extract.

3. Combine flour, nuts, salt and baking powder. Add gradually to creamed mixture at low speed. Beat until well blended.

4. Fit cookie press or pastry bag with desired disk or tip. Fill with dough. Press dough out onto cold baking sheet, forming cookies about 1½ inches apart. (Refrigerate dough about 5 minutes or until firm enough to hold its shape if it becomes too soft.) Sprinkle with colored sugar, if desired.

5. Bake at 350°F for 8 to 10 minutes or until bottoms are light brown. *Do not overbake.* Cool 2 minutes on baking sheet. Remove cookies to foil to cool completely.
Makes about 8 dozen cookies

Swedish Spritz

Buttery Almond Cutouts

1½ cups granulated sugar
1 cup (2 sticks) butter, softened
¾ cup sour cream
2 eggs
3 teaspoons almond extract, divided
1 teaspoon vanilla
4⅓ cups all-purpose flour
1 teaspoon baking powder
1 teaspoon baking soda
½ teaspoon salt
2 cups powdered sugar
2 tablespoons milk
1 tablespoon light corn syrup
Assorted food colorings

1. Beat granulated sugar and butter in large bowl until light and fluffy. Add sour cream, eggs, 2 teaspoons almond extract and vanilla; beat until smooth. Add flour, baking powder, baking soda and salt; beat just until well blended.

2. Divide dough into 4 pieces; flatten each piece into disc. Wrap each disc tightly with plastic wrap. Refrigerate at least 3 hours or up to 3 days.

3. Preheat oven to 375°F. Working with 1 disc of dough at a time, roll out on floured surface to ¼-inch thickness. Cut dough into desired shapes using 2½-inch cookie cutters. Place cutouts about 2 inches apart on ungreased cookie sheets. Bake 7 to 8 minutes or until edges are firm and bottoms are light brown. Remove from cookie sheets to wire racks to cool.

4. Combine powdered sugar, milk, corn syrup and remaining 1 teaspoon almond extract in small bowl; stir until smooth.

5. Divide powdered sugar mixture between 3 or 4 small bowls; tint with desired food coloring. Frost cookies as desired. *Makes about 3 dozen cookies*

Note: To freeze dough, place wrapped discs in resealable plastic food storage bags. Thaw at room temperature before using. Or, cut dough, bake and cool cookies completely. Freeze unfrosted cookies for up to 2 months. Thaw and frost as desired.

Buttery Almond Cutouts

Holiday Cheesecake Presents

  1½ cups HONEY MAID® Graham Cracker Crumbs
  ⅓ cup butter or margarine, melted
  3 tablespoons sugar
  3 packages (8 ounces each) PHILADELPHIA® Cream Cheese, softened
  ¾ cup sugar
  1 teaspoon vanilla
  3 eggs
    Decorating gels
    Colored sprinkles

MIX crumbs, butter and 3 tablespoons sugar; press onto bottom of 13×9-inch baking pan. Beat cream cheese, ¾ cup sugar and vanilla with electric mixer on medium speed until well blended. Add eggs; mix just until blended. Pour over crust.

BAKE at 350°F for 30 minutes or until center is almost set. Cool. Refrigerate 3 hours or overnight. Cut into bars. Decorate with gels and sprinkles to make "presents."

Makes 24 bars

How to Easily Remove Bars From Pan: Line pan with foil before pressing crumb mixture onto bottom of pan.

Green's Mint Meringue Trees

  2 large egg whites
  ¼ teaspoon mint extract
  ½ cup granulated sugar
    Green food coloring
  ½ cup "M&M's"® Semi-Sweet Chocolate Mini Baking Bits

Preheat oven to 250°F. Line baking sheet with parchment paper; set aside. In large bowl beat egg whites until foamy. Add mint extract; beat until soft peaks form. Gradually add sugar; beat until stiff peaks form. Fold in a few drops food coloring to make desired shade of green. Using pastry bag with round or star tip, pipe 3-inch tree shapes onto prepared baking sheet. Decorate with "M&M's"® Semi-Sweet Chocolate Mini Baking Bits. Bake 12 to 15 minutes or until set. Cool on baking sheet 1 minute; cool completely on wire rack. Store in tightly covered container.

Makes 1½ dozen cookies

Holiday Cheesecake Presents

Hershey's Holiday Cookies

2 cups all-purpose flour
½ teaspoon baking soda
¼ teaspoon salt
½ cup (1 stick) butter or margarine, softened
¾ cup packed light brown sugar
½ cup granulated sugar
1 teaspoon vanilla extract
2 eggs
1⅓ cups (10-ounce package) HERSHEY'S Semi-Sweet
Chocolate Holiday Bits, divided
1 cup chopped nuts

1. Heat oven to 350°F. Lightly grease cookie sheet.

2. Stir together flour, baking soda and salt; set aside. Beat butter, brown sugar, granulated sugar and vanilla in large bowl until well blended. Add eggs; beat well. Gradually add flour mixture, beating until well blended. Stir in 1 cup bits and nuts. Drop by rounded teaspoons onto prepared cookie sheet. Press 7 or 8 of remaining bits on each cookie before baking.

3. Bake 9 to 11 minutes or until lightly browned. Cool slightly; remove from cookie sheet to wire rack. Cool completely. *Makes about 3½ dozen cookies*

Hershey's Holiday Cookies

Swedish Sandwich Cookies

1 cup (2 sticks) butter, softened
½ cup plus 2 tablespoons sugar, divided
1 egg yolk
1 egg, separated
2 to 2¼ cups all-purpose flour
3 tablespoons ground almonds
⅔ cup red currant or strawberry jelly

1. Beat butter and ½ cup sugar in large bowl with electric mixer at medium speed until light and fluffy. Beat in 2 egg yolks.

2. Gradually add 1½ cups flour; beat at low speed until well blended. Stir in additional flour with spoon to form stiff dough. Form dough into 2 discs; wrap in plastic wrap and refrigerate until firm, at least 2 hours.

3. Preheat oven to 375°F. Grease and flour cookie sheets. Unwrap 1 disc and place on lightly floured surface. Roll out dough with lightly floured rolling pin to ³⁄₁₆-inch thickness. Cut dough with floured 2¼-inch *round* cookie cutter. Place cutouts 1½ to 2 inches apart on prepared cookie sheets. Gently knead dough trimmings together; reroll and cut out more cookies.

4. Unwrap remaining dough disc and place on lightly floured surface. Roll out dough with lightly floured rolling pin to ³⁄₁₆-inch thickness. Cut dough with floured 2¼-inch *scalloped* cookie cutter. Cut 1-inch centers out of scalloped cookies. Place cutouts 1½ to 2 inches apart on prepared cookie sheets. Cut equal numbers of round and scalloped cookies.

5. Beat egg white in small cup with wire whisk. Combine almonds and remaining 2 tablespoons sugar in small bowl. Brush each scalloped cookie with egg white; sprinkle with sugar mixture. Bake all cookies 8 to 10 minutes or until firm and light golden brown. Remove cookies to wire racks; cool completely.

6. To assemble sandwich cookie, spread about ½ teaspoon currant jelly over flat side of each round cookie; top with flat side of scalloped cookie. Repeat with remaining cookies and jelly. Store tightly covered at room temperature or freeze up to 3 months. *Makes 1½ dozen sandwich cookies*

Cranberry Macadamia Jumbles

1 egg
2 tablespoons MAXWELL HOUSE® Instant Coffee, any variety
½ teaspoon vanilla
½ cup (1 stick) butter or margarine
½ cup granulated sugar
¼ cup firmly packed brown sugar
1 cup flour
1 teaspoon baking soda
¼ teaspoon salt
3 squares BAKER'S® Semi-Sweet Baking Chocolate, chopped
3 squares BAKER'S® Premium White Chocolate, chopped
2 cups macadamia nuts, chopped
1½ cups dried cranberries

HEAT oven to 350°F.

STIR egg, instant coffee and vanilla in small bowl until well blended; set aside.

BEAT butter and sugars in large bowl with electric mixer on medium speed until light and fluffy. Mix in egg mixture. Beat in flour, baking soda and salt on low speed until well blended. Stir in chocolates, nuts and fruit. Drop by rounded tablespoonfuls, 2 inches apart, onto ungreased cookie sheets.

BAKE 10 to 12 minutes or until golden brown. Cool 2 to 3 minutes; remove from cookie sheets. Cool completely on wire racks. Store in tightly covered container.

Makes about 3 dozen cookies

Prep Time: 20 minutes
Bake Time: 12 minutes

Gingerbread People

2¼ cups all-purpose flour
  2 teaspoons ground cinnamon
  2 teaspoons ground ginger
  1 teaspoon baking powder
  ½ teaspoon salt
  ¼ teaspoon ground cloves
  ¼ teaspoon ground nutmeg
  ¾ cup (1½ sticks) butter, softened
  ½ cup packed light brown sugar
  ½ cup dark molasses
  1 egg
    Icing (recipe follows) or prepared creamy or gel-type tube frosting (optional)
    Candies and other decorations (optional)

1. Combine flour, cinnamon, ginger, baking powder, salt, cloves and nutmeg. Beat butter and brown sugar in large bowl until light and fluffy. Beat in molasses and egg. Gradually add flour mixture; beat until well blended. Shape dough into 3 discs. Wrap well in plastic wrap; refrigerate 1 hour or until firm.

2. Preheat oven to 350°F. Working with 1 disc at a time, place on lightly floured surface. Roll out dough with lightly floured rolling pin to ³⁄₁₆-inch thickness. Cut dough into gingerbread people with floured 5-inch cookie cutters; place on ungreased cookie sheets. Press dough trimmings together gently; reroll and cut out more cookies.

3. Bake about 12 minutes or until edges are golden brown. Let cookies stand on cookie sheets 1 minute; remove to wire racks to cool completely.

4. Prepare Icing and pipe onto cooled cookies, if desired. Decorate with candies, if desired. Let stand at room temperature 20 minutes or until set. Store tightly covered at room temperature or freeze up to 3 months. *Makes about 16 large cookies*

Icing

  2 cups powdered sugar
  2 tablespoons milk or lemon juice
    Food coloring (optional)

Blend powdered sugar and milk until smooth. (If necessary, thin icing with additional 1 to 2 teaspoons milk.) Divide into small bowls and tint with food coloring, if desired.

Gingerbread People

Icicle Ornaments

2½ cups all-purpose flour
¼ teaspoon salt
1 cup sugar
¾ cup (1½ sticks) unsalted butter, softened
2 squares (1 ounce each) white chocolate, melted
1 egg
1 teaspoon vanilla
Coarse white decorating sugar, colored sugars and decors
Ribbon

1. Combine flour and salt in medium bowl. Beat sugar and butter in large bowl with electric mixer at medium speed until fluffy. Beat in melted white chocolate, egg and vanilla. Gradually add flour mixture. Beat at low speed until well blended. Shape dough into disc. Wrap in plastic wrap and refrigerate 30 minutes or until firm.

2. Preheat oven to 350°F. Grease cookie sheets. Shape heaping tablespoonfuls of dough into 10-inch ropes. Fold each rope in half; twist to make icicle shape, leaving opening at top and tapering ends. Roll in coarse sugar; sprinkle with colored sugars and decors as desired. Place 1 inch apart on prepared cookie sheets.

3. Bake 8 to 10 minutes. (Do not brown.) Cool on cookie sheets 1 minute. Remove to wire racks; cool completely. Pull ribbon through opening in top of each icicle; tie small knot in ribbon ends. *Makes about 2½ dozen cookies*

Icicle Ornaments

Classic Sugar Cookies

Cookies
    1 cup Butter Flavor CRISCO® All-Vegetable Shortening or
        1 Butter Flavor CRISCO® Stick
  1½ cups granulated sugar
   ½ cup brown sugar
    2 tablespoons milk
    3 eggs
    1 teaspoon vanilla
    4 to 5 cups all-purpose flour
  1½ teaspoons baking soda
  1½ teaspoon cream of tartar
    1 teaspoon salt
    Colored sugars and decors (optional)

Buttery Cream Frosting
    4 cups confectioners' sugar
   ⅓ cup Butter Flavor CRISCO® All-Vegetable Shortening or
        ⅓ Butter Flavor CRISCO® Stick
  1½ teaspoons vanilla
    6 to 7 tablespoons milk
    Food color (optional)

For cookies, combine 1 cup shortening, granulated sugar and brown sugar in large bowl. Beat at medium speed with electric mixer until well blended. Add milk. Beat in eggs, one at a time. Add 1 teaspoon vanilla.

Combine flour, baking soda, cream of tartar and salt. Add to shortening mixture; beat at low speed until well blended. Chill for 1 hour.

Heat oven to 350°F. Roll out ⅓ of dough at a time to about ¼-inch thickness on floured surface. Cut out with cookie cutters. Place 2 inches apart on ungreased baking sheet. Sprinkle with colored sugars and decors or leave plain and frost when cooled.

Bake at 350°F for 5 to 6 minutes or until edges of cookies are slightly golden. Remove cookies immediately to cooling rack. Cool completely before frosting.

For frosting, combine confectioners' sugar, ⅓ cup shortening and 1½ teaspoons vanilla in large bowl. Slowly blend in milk to reach desired consistency. Beat at high speed with electric mixer for 5 minutes or until smooth and creamy. Tint frosting with food color, if desired.   *Makes about 5 dozen cookies*

Classic Sugar Cookies

Jingle Jumbles

¾ cup butter or margarine, softened
1 cup packed brown sugar
¼ cup molasses
1 egg
2¼ cups unsifted all-purpose flour
2 teaspoons baking soda
1 teaspoon ground ginger
1 teaspoon ground cinnamon
½ teaspoon salt
½ teaspoon ground cloves
1¼ cups SUN•MAID® Raisins
Granulated sugar

In large bowl, cream butter and brown sugar. Add molasses and egg; beat until fluffy. In medium bowl, sift together flour, baking soda, ginger, cinnamon, salt and cloves. Stir into molasses mixture. Stir in raisins. Cover and chill about 30 minutes.

Preheat oven to 375°F. Grease cookie sheets. Form dough into 1½-inch balls; roll in granulated sugar, coating generously. Place 2 inches apart on prepared cookie sheets.

Bake 12 to 14 minutes or until edges are firm and centers are still slightly soft. Remove to wire racks to cool. *Makes about 2 dozen cookies*

Jingle Jumbles

Chocolate-Dipped Coconut Macaroons

1 package (14 ounces) BAKER'S® ANGEL FLAKE® Coconut (5⅓ cups)
⅔ cup sugar
6 tablespoons flour
¼ teaspoon salt
4 egg whites
1 teaspoon almond extract
1 package (8 squares) BAKER'S® Semi-Sweet Baking Chocolate, melted

MIX coconut, sugar, flour and salt in large bowl. Add egg whites and almond extract; mix well. Drop by tablespoonfuls onto greased and floured baking sheets.

BAKE at 325°F for 20 minutes or until edges of cookies are golden brown. Immediately remove from baking sheets to wire racks. Cool completely.

DIP cookies halfway into melted chocolate. Let stand at room temperature or refrigerate on wax paper-lined tray 30 minutes or until chocolate is firm. Store tightly covered at room temperature up to 1 week. *Makes about 3 dozen cookies*

Snow-Covered Almond Crescents

1 cup (2 sticks) margarine or butter, softened
¾ cup powdered sugar
½ teaspoon almond extract or 2 teaspoons vanilla extract
2 cups all-purpose flour
¼ teaspoon salt (optional)
1 cup QUAKER® Oats (quick or old fashioned, uncooked)
½ cup finely chopped almonds
Additional powdered sugar

Preheat oven to 325°F. Beat margarine, ¾ cup powdered sugar and almond extract until fluffy. Add flour and salt; mix until well blended. Stir in oats and almonds. Shape level measuring tablespoonfuls of dough into crescents. Place on ungreased cookie sheets about 2 inches apart.

Bake 14 to 17 minutes or until bottoms are light golden brown. Remove to wire racks. Sift additional powdered sugar generously over warm cookies. Cool completely. Store tightly covered. *Makes about 4 dozen cookies*

Chocolate-Dipped Coconut Macaroons

Peanut Butter Chip Tassies

1 package (3 ounces) cream cheese, softened
½ cup (1 stick) butter, softened
1 cup all-purpose flour
½ cup sugar
1 egg, slightly beaten
2 tablespoons butter, melted
¼ teaspoon lemon juice
¼ teaspoon vanilla extract
1 cup REESE'S® Peanut Butter Chips, chopped*
6 red candied cherries, quartered (optional)

Do not chop peanut butter chips in food processor or blender.

1. Beat cream cheese and ½ cup butter in medium bowl; stir in flour. Cover; refrigerate about one hour or until dough is firm. Shape into 24 one-inch balls; place each ball into ungreased small muffin cups (1¾ inches in diameter). Press dough evenly against bottom and side of each cup.

2. Heat oven to 350°F.

3. Combine sugar, egg, melted butter, lemon juice and vanilla in medium bowl; stir until smooth. Add chopped peanut butter chips. Fill muffin cups ¾ full with mixture.

4. Bake 20 to 25 minutes or until filling is set and lightly browned. Cool completely; remove from pan to wire rack. Garnish with candied cherries, if desired.

Makes about 2 dozen

Peanut Butter Chip Tassies

Holiday Triple Chocolate Yule Logs

1¾ cups all-purpose flour
¾ cup powdered sugar
¼ cup unsweetened cocoa powder
⅛ teaspoon salt
1 cup (2 sticks) butter, softened
1 teaspoon vanilla
1 cup white chocolate chips
1 cup chocolate sprinkles or jimmies

1. Combine flour, sugar, cocoa and salt; set aside.

2. Beat butter and vanilla in large bowl with electric mixer at medium-low speed until fluffy. Gradually beat in flour mixture until well blended. Cover and chill dough at least 30 minutes.

3. Preheat oven to 350°F. Form dough into 1-inch balls. Shape balls into 2-inch logs about ½ inch thick. Place 2 inches apart on ungreased cookie sheets.

4. Bake 12 minutes or until set. Let stand on cookie sheets 2 minutes; transfer to wire racks; cool completely.

5. Place white chocolate chips in small microwavable bowl. Microwave at HIGH (100%) 45 seconds. Stir chips until completely melted. Place chocolate sprinkles in another small bowl. Dip each end of cooled cookie first into white chocolate and then into chocolate sprinkles. Return to wire racks; let stand until chocolate is set, about 25 minutes. *Makes about 3 dozen cookies*

Holiday Triple Chocolate Yule Logs

Philadelphia® Snowmen Cookies

1 package (8 ounces) PHILADELPHIA® Cream Cheese, softened
1 cup powdered sugar
¾ cup (1½ sticks) butter or margarine
½ teaspoon vanilla
2 cups flour
½ teaspoon baking soda
    Suggested decorations, such as decorating gels, colored sprinkles, nonpareils and peanut butter cups

MIX cream cheese, sugar, butter and vanilla with electric mixer on medium speed until well blended. Add flour and baking soda; mix well.

SHAPE dough into equal number of ½-inch and 1-inch diameter balls. Using 1 small and 1 large ball for each snowman, place balls, slightly overlapping, on ungreased cookie sheet. Flatten to ¼-inch thickness with bottom of glass dipped in additional flour. Repeat with remaining dough.

BAKE at 325°F for 19 to 21 minutes or until lightly browned. Cool on wire rack. Sprinkle each snowman with sifted powdered sugar. Decorate with decorating gels, colored sprinkles and nonpareils to resemble snowmen. Place 1 candy half on top of each snowman for hats. *Makes about 3 dozen cookies*

Take a Shortcut: To speed-soften cream cheese, unwrap and microwave on HIGH for 10 to 15 seconds.

Prep Time: 20 minutes
Total Time: 41 minutes

Philadelphia® Snowmen Cookies

Holiday Cookies on a Stick

    1 cup (2 sticks) butter or margarine, softened
    ¾ cup granulated sugar
    ¾ cup packed light brown sugar
    1 teaspoon vanilla extract
    2 eggs
2⅓ cups all-purpose flour
    ½ cup HERSHEY'S Cocoa
    1 teaspoon baking soda
    ½ teaspoon salt
    About 18 wooden ice cream sticks
    1 tub (16 ounces) vanilla ready-to-spread frosting (optional)
    Decorating icing in tube, colored sugar, candy sprinkles, HERSHEY'S Semi-Sweet Chocolate Holiday Bits, HERSHEY'S MINI KISSES™ Semi-Sweet or Milk Chocolates

1. Heat oven to 350°F.

2. Beat butter, granulated sugar, brown sugar and vanilla in large bowl on medium speed of mixer until creamy. Add eggs; beat well. Stir together flour, cocoa, baking soda and salt; gradually add to butter mixture, beating until well blended.

3. Drop dough by scant ¼ cupfuls onto ungreased cookie sheet, about 3 inches apart. Shape into balls. Insert wooden stick about three-fourths of the way into side of each ball. Flatten slightly.

4. Bake 8 to 10 minutes or until set. (Cookies will spread during baking.) Cool 3 minutes; using wide spatula, carefully remove from cookie sheet to wire rack. Cool completely.

5. Spread with frosting, if desired. Decorate as desired with Christmas motifs, such as star, tree, candy cane, holly and Santa using decorating icing and garnishes.

Makes about 18 (3½-inch) cookies

Holiday Cookies on a Stick

acknowledgments

The publisher would like to thank the companies and organizations listed below for the use of their recipes and photographs in this publication.

Arm & Hammer Division, Church & Dwight Co., Inc.

Blue Diamond Growers®

ConAgra Foods®

Dole Food Company, Inc.

Domino® Foods, Inc.

Duncan Hines® and Moist Deluxe®
are registered trademarks of Aurora Foods Inc.

Eagle Brand®

Hershey Foods Corporation

Kraft Foods Holdings

© Mars, Incorporated 2004

McIlhenny Company (TABASCO® brand Pepper Sauce)

Mott's® is a registered trademark of Mott's, Inc.

National Honey Board

Nestlé USA

Peanut Advisory Board

The Quaker® Oatmeal Kitchens

The J.M. Smucker Company

Reprinted with permission of Sunkist Growers, Inc.

Sun•Maid® Growers of California

Unilever Bestfoods North America

Walnut Marketing Board

Wisconsin Milk Marketing Board

index

METRIC CONVERSION CHART

VOLUME MEASUREMENTS (dry)

⅛ teaspoon = 0.5 mL
¼ teaspoon = 1 mL
½ teaspoon = 2 mL
¾ teaspoon = 4 mL
1 teaspoon = 5 mL
1 tablespoon = 15 mL
2 tablespoons = 30 mL
¼ cup = 60 mL
⅓ cup = 75 mL
½ cup = 125 mL
⅔ cup = 150 mL
¾ cup = 175 mL
1 cup = 250 mL
2 cups = 1 pint = 500 mL
3 cups = 750 mL
4 cups = 1 quart = 1 L

VOLUME MEASUREMENTS (fluid)

1 fluid ounce (2 tablespoons) = 30 mL
4 fluid ounces (½ cup) = 125 mL
8 fluid ounces (1 cup) = 250 mL
12 fluid ounces (1½ cups) = 375 mL
16 fluid ounces (2 cups) = 500 mL

WEIGHTS (mass)

½ ounce = 15 g
1 ounce = 30 g
3 ounces = 90 g
4 ounces = 120 g
8 ounces = 225 g
10 ounces = 285 g
12 ounces = 360 g
16 ounces = 1 pound = 450 g

DIMENSIONS

1/16 inch = 2 mm
⅛ inch = 3 mm
¼ inch = 6 mm
½ inch = 1.5 cm
¾ inch = 2 cm
1 inch = 2.5 cm

OVEN TEMPERATURES

250°F = 120°C
275°F = 140°C
300°F = 150°C
325°F = 160°C
350°F = 180°C
375°F = 190°C
400°F = 200°C
425°F = 220°C
450°F = 230°C

BAKING PAN SIZES

Utensil	Size in Inches/Quarts	Metric Volume	Size in Centimeters
Baking or Cake Pan (square or rectangular)	8×8×2	2 L	20×20×5
	9×9×2	2.5 L	23×23×5
	12×8×2	3 L	30×20×5
	13×9×2	3.5 L	33×23×5
Loaf Pan	8×4×3	1.5 L	20×10×7
	9×5×3	2 L	23×13×7
Round Layer Cake Pan	8×1½	1.2 L	20×4
	9×1½	1.5 L	23×4
Pie Plate	8×1¼	750 mL	20×3
	9×1¼	1 L	23×3
Baking Dish or Casserole	1 quart	1 L	—
	1½ quart	1.5 L	—
	2 quart	2 L	—